Gann Simplified

By Clif Droke

MARKETPLACE BOOKS
Columbia, MD

MARKETPLACE BOOKS

Simplified Series

Technical Analysis Simplified *by Clif Droke*

Elliott Wave Simplified *by Clif Droke*

Moving Averages Simplified *by Clif Droke*

Gann Simplified *by Clif Droke*

Other ground-breaking books in the Marketplace Books Series:

The Precision Profit Float Indicator: Powerful Techniques to Exploit Price and Volume *by Steve Woods*

Trader's Guide to Technical Analysis *by C. Colburn Hardy*

Commodity Options: Spectacular Options with Limited Risk *by Larry Spears*

Trend Forecasting: Unleashing the Hidden Power of Intermarket Analysis to Beat the Market *by Louis B. Mendelsohn*

7 Chart Patterns That Consistently Make Money *by Ed Downs*

Trading, Sex, and Dying: The Heart of a Gambler *by Juel E. Anderson*

The ARMS Index *by Richard Arms, Jr.*

The New Market Wizards: Conversations with America's Top Traders *by Jack D. Schwager*

McMillan on Options *by Lawrence G. McMillan*

The Art of Short Selling *by Kathryn Staley*

Point and Figure Charting: Essential Applications for Forecasting and Tracking Market Prices *by Tom Dorsey*

The Trader's Tax Solution: Money Saving Strategies for the Serious Investor *by Ted Tesser*

"If you make speculation or investment a business, you probably will be able to accumulate a fortune over a number of years, but if you go into it to gamble and expect to make it all on one deal, you will lose all your money and have nothing left but hope."

—W.D. Gann,
How to Make Profits in Commodities

This book, along with other books, are available at discounts that make it realistic to provide them as gifts to your customers, clients and staff. For more information on these long-lasting, cost-effective premiums, please call John Boyer at 800-272-2855 or e-mail him at john@traderslibrary.com.

ISBN 1-931611-24-6

Printed in the United States of America

Contents

Foreword

What is it that makes the writings of W.D. Gann so fascinating, yet still controversial to so many? Are there, contained within his writings, specific ideas that unlock the Holy Grail of the stock market and change the way you look at price and volume charts? Can he really help you become a better investor or trader?

All serious students of the stock market are eventually drawn to the writings of W.D. Gann and Clif Droke's book is an excellent place to start.

Many deeply believe so. In fact, Gann's writings and concepts are embraced by scores of serious investors and professional traders, to this day. And some of those investors have found, as I have, that his writings have significantly influenced their trading in a very positive way. I can emphatically state that more than any other person, the writings of W.D. Gann have completely changed my approach to the stock market. Using his ideas, I was able to increase, by tenfold, a small portfolio of several thousand dollars, over a period of sixteen months.

It was in Gann's book, *Truth of the Stock Tape*, that I came across the idea that changed the way I personally looked at price and volume charts, by comparing a stock's cumulative trading volume to its floating supply of shares. The impact of this idea was like the cliché of "getting hit with a ton of bricks" and here is why: I had observed several dozen high-flying stocks as they came crashing down to earth. It was Gann's teachings that made me realize that if there was a rectangular distance on a chart in which the cumulative volume equaled the floating supply of shares, then that rectangle represented a proxy for a change in ownership in that company. I then reasoned that a change in ownership most likely would occurr right at the top and that the rectangle could always be seen as the place of final distribution. The implication of these ideas led me to realize that there would also be a rectangular area at long-term bottoms, which could be seen as the place of initial accumulation.

W.D. Gann had an enormous impact on my approach to the stock market, and it was his direct influence which led me to conclude that the number of shares available for trading was *as important* as price and volume, and that viewing stocks in this way could reveal accumulation bottoms and distribution tops.

At that time I did not own a computer and charted stocks entirely by hand. With Gann's ideas resonating in my head, I began the laborious task of tracking the float turnover for a large number of stocks. Adding volume numbers cumulatively and comparing them to a stock's float was quite difficult and could take hours, even with a handheld calculator. But the end result of this intense study convinced me that my thoughts on the subject were exactly right. I then purchased a computer and hired a systems analyst to write the cumulative-volume float indicator that is documented in my book, *The Precision Profit Float Indicator*. In short, W.D. Gann had an enormous impact on my approach to the stock market, and it was his direct influence which led me to conclude that the number of shares available for trading was *as important* as price and volume, and that viewing stocks in this way could reveal accumulation bottoms and distribution tops.

When I first read Clif Droke's manuscript for this book, I had not read any of Gann's material in quite some time. I found the experience of revisiting Gann's work *more* than enjoyable. There is something about Gann's material that is akin to reading an ancient manuscript that talks of turning ordinary stones into gold. It is as though one has discovered the actual writings of Merlin.

I truly believe that many of Gann's ideas are timeless and stand as a testament to a man who spent his life studying the markets, successfully trading them, and sharing his ideas with others. His teachings have stood the test of time and are regarded as one of the foundations of financial research. After reading his work, one gets the impression that Gann had seen it all and understood the importance of sharing his discoveries. Yet, there is also the feeling that his *most* important discoveries were not fully revealed — and may still be shrouded in some secret code, which has yet to be uncovered. Perhaps new students of Gann techniques will finally be able to unlock the code — and reveal even more of Gann's impressive body of work.

Those new to Gann's methods should find *Gann Simplified* a fascinating introduction. Clif Droke has done an excellent job of delivering the "essence" of W.D. Gann's writings. He not only gives the reader the best of Gann's ideas in Gann's own words, but also elaborates on Gann's teachings in a clear and easy-to-follow style.

Clif Droke has done an excellent job of delivering the "essence" of W.D. Gann's writings. He not only gives the reader the best of Gann's ideas in Gann's own words, but also elaborates on Gann's teachings in a clear and easy-to-follow style.

Likewise, even those who have read Gann in the past will find this new book stimulating. Readers will learn that much of the wisdom from today's top "gurus" originally came from Gann. *Gann Simplified* also presents essential writings on Gann angles, the Law of Vibration, swing charts, reading the tape, the "24 never failing rules," the dangers of over-trading, how much to risk on any one trade, using stop loss orders, the importance of weekly, monthly and quarterly charts, and much more.

Even those who have read Gann in the past will find this new book stimulating.

If in reading any book on the stock market I can uncover one nugget of information that will either make me money or save me from losing it, then I feel that my money was well spent. This book certainly meets that criteria and I highly recommend it.

— Steve Woods,
Author of *The Precision Profit Float Indicator*

CHAPTER 1

W.D. Gann:

The Man and His Incredible Trading Legacy

The name of W.D. Gann has become legendary among traders and market technicians today. Tales of his phenomenal success in trading and his arcane, yet highly accurate, technical theories are widely known. Not so well known, however, are the particulars about Gann and his methods. Who was this mysterious man who claimed to have discovered the secrets of consistently and accurately forecasting the markets? What discoveries enabled him to do this? Do his theories and techniques still apply in today's markets? More importantly, if they do still apply, can they be explained in a straight-forward, simplistic manner without the esoteric jargon and abstruse mathematical concepts that enshroud much of his work?

W.D. Gann. Photo courtesy of Lambert Gann Publishing, Pomeroy, Washington

To begin, let's explore a little of Gann's background. William Delbert Gann was born on a cotton ranch on June 6, 1878, in Lufkin, Texas. He displayed a strong aptitude in mathematics during his early years, completed a high-school education, and started trading in 1902 at the age of 24. By his own admission, Gann's early trading was based on "hope, fear and greed," all of which he later realized were not compatible with a successful trading strategy.[1]

"After losing significant sums of money," writes James A. Hyerczyk in his excellent work on Gann theory entitled *Pattern, Price & Time,*[2] "Gann began to observe that markets followed mathematical laws and certain time cycles. He was particularly interested in the connection between price and time, a relationship he referred to as the 'square' of price and time. He began studying this interaction diligently, even traveling to England, India, and Egypt to research mathematical theory and historical prices.

"In developing his theories, Gann was undoubtedly one of the most industrious technical analysts. He made thousands of charts displaying daily, weekly, monthly and yearly prices for a wide variety of stocks and commodities. He was an avid researcher, occasionally charting a price back hundreds of years. At a time when most market analysis was strictly fundamental, Gann's revolutionary theories relied on natural laws of mathematics, time cycles, and his unshakeable conviction that past market activity predicted future activity."[3]

In conducting his market research, Gann discovered a rule that would become the bedrock of his trading methodology, a rule he called the "Law of Vibration," which he claimed applied to the realm of natural science as well as the financial realm. *Gann so refined this law that once a stock started to move higher or lower he was able to pinpoint the exact level to which a stock would rise or fall, and often the exact time required to reach this objective.* He is famous, of course, for being one of the few to accurately forecast the stock market crash of 1929 and subsequent depression. In fact, he wrote a detailed month-by-month overview and forecast for the entire trading year 1929 one full year in advance (as part of his "Annual Stock Forecast" service to his newsletter subscribers); the vast majority of which was accurately fulfilled.

Gann was as versatile a trader as he was a successful one. Unlike traders of today who tend to specialize in a single area (like stocks or particular commodities), Gann made money trading in everything. He was a member of the New York Rubber Exchange, New York Commodity Exchange, New Orleans Cotton Exchange, and Chicago Board of Trade. In his various books he describes his methods for accurately forecasting price trends of a wide variety of commodities, including coffee, sugar, cocoa, rubber, hides, hogs, eggs, cotton, wheat, rye, corn, soybeans, wool, lard, and butter. If there was an exchange for it, Gann probably traded it, regardless of what it was. This goes to show the universality of Gann's phenomenal trading and forecasting techniques, which can be applied to any market.

By all indications, Gann's trading success was impressive. According to Hyerczyk, an analysis of Gann's trading record over 25 market days revealed that Gann made 286 trades, 264 of which were profitable. His success rate of 92.31% turned an initial investment of $450 into $37,000. [4] It has been rumored that over the span of his trading career, Gann acquired cumulative profits totaling $50 million, a figure which, however, is unsubstantiated.

Gann so refined his "Law of Vibration," that once a stock started to move higher or lower he was able to pinpoint the exact level to which a stock would rise or fall, and often the exact time required to reach this objective.

Brokerage statements indicate that he traded an account with a balance in excess of $2 million[5] and that upon his death he left an estate valued at around $5 million.

During his lifetime, Gann generously shared his knowledge and ideas with others, penning a total of seven books and numerous trading courses. Most of his more complex, intricate techniques were revealed in his commodity trading courses, such as the "Master Egg Course," among others. But the basis of his theories was revealed in more down-to-earth, perpetually popular volumes such as *Truth of the Stock Tape* and its companion, *Wall Street Stock Selector*. Other works include *The Tunnel Thru the Air: Or, Looking Back from 1940*; *New Stock Trend Indicator*; *How to Make Profits in Commodities*; and *45 Years in Wall Street*.

Overall, W.D. Gann was arguably one of the most successful and accurate traders in the annals of Wall Street history. He set world records for leverage and trading profits on more than one occasion, and unlike most of his successful peers, he never failed to share his knowledge with an eager trading public, desirous of learning the proper way to acquire profits in the markets. He was as prolific and successful a teacher as he was a trader, a legacy which endures even today, as many of the world's top traders and investors continue to pore through his work and adapt Gann methods to modern-day instruments. Let us now take a look at some of the basic princi- ples of Gann Theory, which continue to influence modern-day investors.

NOTES

1 Hyerczyk, James A., *Pattern, Price & Time: Using Gann Theory in Trading Systems*, John Wiley & Sons, 1998, pg. 1

2 Ibid., pg. 1

3 Ibid., pg. 1

4 Ibid., pg. 2

5 Ibid., pg. 3

CHAPTER 2

The Foundations of Gann Theory

The Basics: Pattern, Price and Time

The three basic concerns of Gann theory are pattern, price and time. By "pattern" Gann meant identifiable and recurrent price formations in charts of stocks and commodities. Gann taught that these patterns could be recognized time and again, and could be used to forecast price movements since these various patterns always tend to repeat.

Gann also placed special emphasis on "price," by which he meant that a trader should constantly focus on the price of the stock or commodity itself. Gann had several ways of doing this. He taught his students to compare the current price of a stock or commodity to its previous high or low price in order to get an indication of where it was in the trading range (a trading range is a concept that will be more fully explained in a later chapter). He also taught that a chart should be divided up into percentages from one significant top to a significant bottom, placing special emphasis on the 50% portion of the divided range. Percentages were also a big part of his technique. As a student of geometry, Gann even taught

By "pattern" Gann meant identifiable and recurrent price formations in charts of stocks and commodities. Gann also placed special emphasis on "price," by which he meant that a trader should constantly focus on the price of the stock or commodity itself.

that the geometric angle at which the price of a stock or commodity is positioned on a chart has meaning (another concept we'll discuss later on).

Finally, Gann emphasized "time" in the study of market. In fact, he considered the time element to be of the greatest importance, since time is the least common denominator in the equation of the marketplace and is the only constant factor in the study of all kinds of markets. A great deal of Gann's work was centered on the study of time cycles, seasonal trends, and historical dates. Gann gave special weighting and consideration to each of these three basic factors at different times, depending on the market environment in which he was trading. He believed that each of the three factors dominated at various times.

Role of Scientific Law

Gann considered the key to his success a theory he formulated based on his study of scientific laws and his observation of the laws governing the motion of bodies, which he called the "Law of Vibration." He insisted that this scientific law governed the motion of everything from humans to planets, and could also be seen in the marketplace. He described his discovery of this law in detail in an interview he gave to Richard D. Wyckoff, editor of *The Magazine of Wall Street*, in the early 1900s. Part of that interview is excerpted below:

"I soon began to note the periodical recurrence of the rise and fall in stocks and commodities. This led me to conclude that natural law was the basis of market movements. After exhaustive researches and investigations of the known sciences, I discovered that the Law of Vibration enables me to accurately determine the exact points to which stocks or commodities should rise and fall within a given time. The working out of this law determines the cause, and predicts the effect, long before the Street is aware of either. Most speculators can testify to the fact that it is looking at the effect and ignoring the cause that has produced their losses . . .

"It is impossible to give an adequate idea of the Law of Vibration as I apply it to the markets; however, the layman may be able to grasp some of the principles when I state that the Law of Vibration is the fundamental law upon which wireless telegraphy, wireless telephone and phonographs are based. Without the existence of the law the above inventions would have been impossible . . .

"In going over the history of markets and the great mass of related statistics, it soon becomes apparent that certain laws govern the changes and variations in the value of stocks and there exists a period of cyclic law, which is at the back of all these movements. Observation has shown that there are regular periods of intense activity on the Exchange followed by periods of inactivity. . . . The law which I have applied will not only give these long cycles or swings, but the daily and even hourly movements of stocks. By knowing the exact vibration of each individual stock I am able to determine at what point each will receive support and at what point the greatest resistance is to be met . . .

Gann considered the key to his success a theory he formulated based on his study of scientific laws and his observation of the laws governing the motion of bodies, which he called the "Law of Vibration."

After exhaustive researches and investigations of the known sciences, I discovered that the Law of Vibration enables me to accurately determine the exact points to which stocks or commodities should rise and fall within a given time. The working out of this law determines the cause and predicts the effect long before the Street is aware of either.

"Those in close touch with the markets have noticed the phenomena of ebb and flow, or rise and fall in the value of stocks. At certain times a stock becomes intensely active, large transactions being made in it; at other times this same stock will become practically stationary or inactive with a very small volume of sales. I have found that the Law of Vibration governs and controls these conditions. I have also found that certain phases of this law govern the rise in a stock and entirely different rules operate on the decline. I have found that in the stock itself exists its harmonic or inharmonic relationship to the driving power or force behind it...

"Science teaches 'that an original impulse of any kind finally resolves itself into periodic or rhythmical motion,' also, 'just as the pendulum returns again in its swing, just as the moon returns in its orbit, just as the advancing year ever brings the rose to spring, so do the properties of the elements periodically recur as the weight of the atom rises...'

"From my exhaustive investigations, studies and applied tests, I find that not only do the various stocks vibrate, but that the driving forces controlling the stocks are also in the state of vibration. These vibratory forces can only be known by the movements they generate on the stocks and their values in the market. Since all great swings or movements of the market are cyclic they act in accordance with the periodic law...

"If we wish to avert failure in speculation we must deal with causes. Everything in existence is based on exact proportion and perfect relationships. There is no chance in nature, because mathematical principles of the highest order lie at the foundation of all things. Faraday said: 'There is nothing in the Universe but mathematical points of force.'. . .

"Through the Law of Vibration every stock in the market moves in its own distinctive sphere of activities, as to intensity, volume and direction; all the essential qualities of its evolution are characterized in its own rate of vibration. Stocks, like atoms, are really centers of energies, therefore they are controlled mathematically. Stocks create their own field of action and power; power to attract and repel, which in principle explains why certain stocks at times lead the market and 'turn dead' at other times. Thus to speculate scientifically it is absolutely necessary to follow natural laws."[1]

Gann: The Mathematician

Gann possessed an extraordinary gift for mathematics. He was a mathematician by nature, so it only followed that much of his technical theory should be concerned with numbers and with mathematical relationships in the markets. Certain numbers took on a special significance in his work, namely, 16, 25, 36, 49, 64, 121, and 144. His numerical theory of the market was based on his study of the Bible, along with ancient Egyptian number theory.

He found, for instance, that the number 7 had a special significance in the Bible and thereby used it to develop a seven-day cycle theory for the short-term study of the market. He considered the number 7 to represent completeness; therefore, seven to him

Stocks, like atoms, are really centers of energies, therefore they are controlled mathematically. Stocks create their own field of action and power; power to attract and repel, which in principle explains why certain stocks at times lead the market and 'turn dead' at other times. Thus to speculate scientifically it is absolutely necessary to follow natural laws."

symbolized time and rhythm, as well as the complete cycle — the basis of Gann theory.

He also considered the half-cycle of 3½ to be vitally important in his study of the markets. The number 7 is a harmonic of 3½. This number is also quite prominent in the Bible and is mentioned, among other places, as being the timeframe of Daniel's vision (3½ years); the time of Christ's public ministry on earth (3½ years); as well as the hiding of the Christ child in Egypt for 3½ years. Thus, Gann used this to formulate a theory demonstrating the existence of a 3½-day, -week, -month, and -year cycle. He applied this knowledge in trading the markets.

Gann possessed an extraordinary gift for mathematics. He was a mathematician by nature, so it only followed that much of his technical theory should be concerned with numbers and with mathematical relationships in the markets.

The number 12 also took on a special significance for Gann as it denoted for him the concept of space. Twelve is also considered to be the reference point of the cycle, since a cycle geometrically represented is a circle, which is composed of 360 degrees. Since there are 12 divisions of the circle of time (i.e., the clock), 12 months in a year, 12 houses in the zodiac, etc., the number 360 divided by 12 yields 30, a number which, besides being the number of days in a month, was important in Gann's trading strategy. Gann posited the existence of a 30-day, 30-month and 30-year trading cycle based on the study of this number.

The number 144 (which is a product of 12 times 12) was also important for Gann, the number also representing the number of minutes in a day (1440, with zero at the end being disregarded). The number 144 also recurs throughout the Bible, and therefore took on an even greater significance for him.

JANUARY	FEBRUARY	MARCH	APRIL	MAY	JUNE	JULY	AUGUST	SEPTEMBER	OCTOBER	NOVEMBER	DECEMBER
365	31	59	90	120	151	181	212	243	273	304	334
334	365	28	59	89	120	150	181	212	242	273	303
306	337	365	31	61	92	122	153	184	214	245	275
275	306	334	365	30	61	91	122	153	183	214	244
245	276	304	335	365	31	61	92	123	153	184	214
214	245	273	304	334	365	30	61	92	122	153	183
184	215	243	274	304	335	365	31	62	92	125	183
153	184	212	243	273	304	334	365	31	61	92	122
122	153	181	212	242	273	303	334	365	30	61	91
92	123	151	182	212	243	273	304	335	365	31	61
61	92	120	151	181	212	242	273	304	334	365	30
31	62	90	121	151	182	212	243	274	304	335	365

Certain numbers, for example 12 and 144 (144 being a product of 12 times 12), took on a special significance in his work. This grid is an example of the type of mathematical relationship he would use in developing a trading strategy.

Based on his many years of studying number theory, then, he concluded that markets adhere to mathematical law. From this conclusion he was able to develop his trading theory. This theory basically stated that market movement is governed by the forces of pattern, price, and time.[2]

Time: The Strongest Market Influence

According to Gann, time had the strongest influence on the market because when time is up, the trend changes.[3] Concerning the importance Gann assigned to the time factor, consider the following Gann quote, in reference to his analysis of the October Eggs futures contract:

"The greatest time period from January 24 to February 8 was 11 market days. And the last advance from April 18 was 11 market days; therefore, when the market declines more than 11 days, it will overbalance the greatest time period. When it declines more than 75 points it will overbalance the last price declines or space reversal, and indicate lower prices."[4]

Notice that Gann used the term "overbalance [of] time." This was a common expression of Gann's in his market writings, and forms an integral part of his theory of technical analysis. Overbalance occurs when a move in price and time overextends and travels too far in one direction. When this happens, the market can be expected to react in the opposite direction with the same force and magnitude, including the time factor. This confers a certain amount of predictability in the movements of prices once this concept has been mastered.

> "Overbalance" occurs when a move in price and time overextends and travels too far in one direction. When this happens, the market can be expected to react in the opposite direction with the same force and magnitude, including the time factor. This confers a certain amount of predictability in the movements of prices once this concept has been mastered.

Combining time and price forms the basis for much of Gann theory. Writes John Murphy, in *Technical Analysis of the Futures Markets*, "Gann saw a definite proportional relationship between the two. One of his methods for finding tops or bottoms is based on the squaring of price and time — that is, when a unit of price equals a unit of time. For example, Gann would take a prominent high in a market, convert that dollar figure into a calendar unit (days, weeks, months, or years), and project that time period forward. When that time period is reached, time and price are squared and a market turn due. As an illustration, if a market hit a prominent high at $100,

Gann counted 100 days, weeks, months, or years forward. Those future dates identified possible turning points."[5]

Among the timing tools Gann used is a concept he referred to as "anniversary dates." This term refers to the historical dates the market made major tops and bottoms. The information collected in effect reflects the seasonality of the market because often an anniversary date repeats in the future. A cluster of anniversary dates indicates the strong tendency of a market to post a major top and bottom each year at the same time.[6] The dates and time spans between these anniversary dates — top to top, top to bottom, bottom to bottom, and bottom to top — were fundamental factors in his thinking.[7] And these relationships further led to his development of theories of time cycles in his quest to accurately forecast price movements in the market.

In his book, *Pattern, Price & Time*, James A. Hyerczyk wrote concerning Gann's time cycle studies, "When looking at anniversary dates he saw a series of one-year cycles. In geometric terms, the one-year cycle represented a circle or 360 degrees. Building on the geometric relationship of the market, Gann also considered the quarterly divisions of the year to be important timing periods. These quarterly divisions are the 90-day cycle, the 180-day cycle, and the 270-day cycle. In using the one-year cycle and the divisions of this cycle, you will find a date where a number of these cycles line up (preferably three or more) in a single point in time in the future. A date where a number of cycles line up is called a *time cluster*.

Combining time and price forms the basis for much of Gann theory. Some of the methods and timing tools used in his analysis for finding tops or bottoms included: squaring of price and time, anniversary dates, time clusters, and time cycles.

This time cluster is used to predict major tops and bottoms. Time cycles are a major part of Gann analysis, and should be combined with price indicators to develop a valid market forecast."[8]

In the chapters that follow we will explain the specifics of applying Gann's methods for predicting price movements in terms of time, price, and pattern. However, one must first understand the concept of tape reading, which Gann felt was very important and this is the subject of our next chapter.

NOTES

1 Hyerczyk, James A., *Pattern, Price & Time: Using Gann Theory in Trading Systems,* John Wiley & Sons Inc., 1998, pgs. 9-11, as reprinted in *The W.D. Gann Technical Review,* vol. 1, no. 11, p. 1, November 12, 1982.

2 Ibid., pg. 13

3 Ibid., pg. 15

4 Gann, W.D., *Truth of the Stock Tape,* Lambert Gann Publishing, Pomeroy, Washington, 1923, pg. 61

5 Murphy, John, *Technical Analysis of the Futures Markets,* New York Institute of Finance, 1986, pg. 538

6 Hyerczyk, pg. 16

7 Ibid., pg. 16

8 Ibid., pg. 16

CHAPTER 3

The Truth of the Stock Tape

Interpreting Price & Volume

G ann laid heavy emphasis on being able to read the tape correctly as a prerequisite for speculative success. Much of his early work focuses on the technique of what was then called "tape reading," i.e., the science of interpreting price and volume in a stock or commodity on a minute-by-minute, hour-by-hour, or day-by-day basis. Most traders and investors pay attention only to price movements, ignoring trading volume. Gann, however, believed that price was only half the picture — trading volume was the other half, and he believed that trading success hinged on being able to put the two together into one comprehensive picture to be able to interpret the balance of supply and demand in a given stock or commodity.

"The tape is the great scale in which the weight of all buying and selling is weighed and the balance of supply and demand shown by the loss or gain in prices," wrote Gann in his seminal work, *Truth of the Stock Tape*. "When supply exceeds demand, prices decline to a level where supply and demand

Most traders and investors pay attention only to price movements, ignoring trading volume. Gann believed that trading success hinged on being able to put the two together into one comprehensive picture to be able to interpret the balance of supply and demand in a given stock or commodity.

are about equal. At this stage fluctuations become narrow and it may require weeks or months to determine which way the next move will be. When demand exceeds supply, prices advance."[1]

Volume of trade alone was a subject Gann assigned great importance to. "Market movements depend on supply and demand," he wrote. "It requires volume of trading in proportionate large or small amounts to move stocks up or down. The volume of sales to the stock market is the same as the steam is to the locomotive or the gasoline is to the automobile. The sales are the motive power which drives prices up or down."[2]

Gann used U.S. Steel, which was one of his favorite stocks to trade in, as an example to illustrate this truth. In his day, U.S. Steel often had five-million shares of common stock outstanding, and it required a very large volume of sales to move this stock up or down to any noticeable degree. General Motors, another of Gann's favorite trading stocks, frequently had fifty-million shares of common stock outstanding and its fluctuations were confined to a very narrow range. Gann pointed out that this was because the buying or selling of 100,000 shares will not move it more than a point, if that much, due to the enormous amount of shares outstanding. Yet another stock popular among traders in Gann's day was Baldwin Locomotive, which had far fewer shares outstanding than General Motors—only about 200,000 shares. The buying of 100,000 shares of Baldwin Locomotive was often sufficient to move it up or down five or ten points due to the thin volume.

"Market movements depend on supply and demand. It requires volume of trading in proportionate large or small amounts to move stocks up or down. The volume of sales to the stock market is the same as the steam is to the locomotive or the gasoline is to the automobile. The sales are the motive power which drives prices up or down."

"Therefore," wrote Gann, "in order to understand the meaning of volume, you must know the total capital stock outstanding and the floating supply of the stock you are trading in." [3]

This concept of comparing total stock outstanding to trading volume was a unique concept that Gann was famous for. More recently, the concept has been revised and discussed in greater detail by Steve Woods, in his book *Precision Profit Float Indicator* (Marketplace Books).

Another thing Gann felt was necessary for tape-reading success was to know the financial position of the stock you were trading in, whether it was in a weak or strong position. "It is not easy to frighten investors and traders and start a selling move in a stock which is generally known to be in a very strong financial position," he wrote. "Neither is it easy to force a stock by manipulation to very high levels that is generally known to have very little intrinsic value." [4]

Another thing Gann felt was necessary for tape-reading success was to know the financial position of the stock you were trading in, whether it was in a weak or strong position.

Time Cycles Govern Price Movements

Time was another element Gann deemed essential to successful speculation. Watching the ticker hour after hour tends to lock the trader into the habit of viewing price and volume movements as the only variable in the supply/demand equation; he often forgets that the only constant variable in any stock or commodity is time, and that furthermore, price movements are governed by time cycles. "It requires time to buy a large amount of stock when accumulation is taking place, and it requires time to distribute a large amount of stock at the top. One day, one week, or one month is not long enough for a big move. Sometimes it requires several months, or even a year, to complete accumulation or distribution. While the process is going on, you can keep up a chart of the stock you are interested in and judge much better when the big move starts, than you can by watching the ticker every day." [5]

This observation led Gann to establish a fundamental rule for reading the tape: "The best way to read the tape correctly is to stay away from it." Even though Gann believed the tape to contain all the information necessary to confer enormous profits to those who learned to read it, he also believed that incessantly watching the tape, reading its quotations constantly, tends to provide a misleading picture of the overall supply/demand balance to most traders. Traders who spend all their time hunched over the ticker (or computer screen as the case may be), in their zeal to trade every minor fluctuation, often become confused as to the much more important larger trend, which is where the big money is usually made. Gann likened this failing to someone trying to admire a painting by a Renaissance master: in looking to closely and too hard at every little brush stroke, one misses the true beauty and elegance of the picture, which can only be seen from a distance. The closer one stands to the painting, the less likely he is to capture the overall symmetry of it. In like manner, the more often one pores over the ticker, obsessed with each minor fluctuation, the less likely he will be able to identify the larger pattern in the supply/demand picture.

Even though Gann believed the tape to contain all the information necessary to confer enormous profits to those who learned to read it, he also believed that incessantly watching the tape, reading its quotations constantly, tends to provide a misleading picture of the overall supply/demand balance to most traders.

Gann often said that the tape is used to fool traders, for often when stocks look the weakest on the tape, they are the strongest as accumulation is taking place. At other times, when they are booming and very active and appear the strongest, they are really at their weakest point, because the insiders are selling while everybody else is enthusiastically buying.

A corollary to this truth is that the biggest mistake a chronic tape watcher makes is that he trades too often, getting in and out sometimes during the day, and each time paying a commission. If he buys or sells higher or lower each time, even though he has made profits on his trades, he is increasing the percentage against him.

It was also emphasized by Gann that the more frequently one trades, the more often one's underlying opinion must change and as a result there is a greater probability that the trader will be wrong. Even in the most dramatic bull or bear markets there are significant moves against the main trend, but day-to-day trading is not the way to capitalize on these movements. Instead, Gann felt that one should have patience and wait until there is a real justification before taking a position. By trying to catch every minor swing, the trader will often miss the major move when it occurs. Daily fluctuations are generally of little importance to the major trend of the market.

Gann felt that one should have patience and wait until there is a real justification before taking a position. By trying to catch every minor swing, the trader will often miss the major move when it occurs. Daily fluctuations are generally of little importance to the major trend of the market.

"This same rule and reasoning should be applied to any other stock you wish to determine the trend of. During the period of accumulation or distribution, the man who tries to read the tape must get fooled dozens of times and make mistakes in trying to follow minor moves which do not mean anything. Therefore, the correct way to read the tape is to keep up a chart showing moves of from three days to one week and the amount of volume. Of course, you must consider the total outstanding stock and the floating supply. Again, I emphasize the fact that the correct way to read the tape and interpret it accurately is to stay away from it."[6]

The point Gann was making in emphasizing all of this is that the trader or investor should keep a daily, weekly, and/or monthly chart of the price and volume history of whatever stock or commodity he happens to be trading in. This pictorial history of the "tape" is the key to successful speculation. Being able to properly read financial charts, more than anything else, was the secret of Gann's trading success. Fortunately, he revealed many of his secrets for interpreting charts in his books, many of which you will learn here.

The Tape Tells All

In revealing his secrets for tape reading, Gann often used the phrase "truth of the stock tape," or repeated the old adage, "the tape tells all." He wrote that the stock market is an accurate barometer of business conditions, with stock prices being nearly always six to twelve months ahead of general business conditions. He noted the following hierarchy of financial developments: first, bond prices rise; second, stocks advance; third, comes business boom. The same order is true in a decline. Stocks will be

The trader or investor should keep a daily, weekly, and/or monthly chart of the price and volume history of whatever stock or commodity he happens to be trading in. This pictorial history of the "tape" is the key to successful speculation. Being able to properly read financial charts, more than anything else, was the secret of Gann's trading success.

down six to eight months while business is booming, because stocks are discounting the future business depression.

"Market movements," wrote Gann, "that is, the
main swings, are the result or effect of causes
which, as a rule, exist long before the effect is
known to the general public. In most cases, news is
discounted before it comes out and seldom has
much effect after it is generally known. Either good
or bad news that is expected usually falls flat as far
as the effect on the market is concerned.

"For instance, an extremely good or bad quarterly or
annual report on a stock comes out and the market
does not go up or down on it for the reason that it
is not news to those on the inside. They knew it
thirty to ninety days beforehand. Therefore, when
the public gets the news and acts on it, it is too late,
for those on the inside who 'know' have already discounted it."[7]

A discussion of Gann's tape-reading technique would not be complete without explaining his method of knowing when to buy or sell a stock, based on indications from the chart or tape. The key to this is knowing how to identify points of accumulation or distribution.

A discussion of Gann's tape-reading technique
would not be complete without explaining his
method of knowing when to buy or sell a stock,
based on indications from the chart or tape. The key
to this is knowing how to identify points of accumulation or distribution. Gann continually emphasized
that the truth that the stock tape has to tell cannot
be told in one day, one week, or one month. It
begins to tell its story the first day that a stock
reaches the buying or selling zone, but it requires
time to complete the story, to assemble all of the
facts, to finish the accumulation or distribution and
give the final signal that a new move is on.

According to
Gann, the length
of time, as well
as the total
number of points
that a stock has
moved up or
down from
high or low
levels, must be
considered in
judging whether
accumulation
or distribution
is taking place.

For example, a stock making a new high would ordi-
narily be an indication that it was going higher, but
after a stock advances into new territory, if it is going
higher, it will continue up without breaking back
below the old top levels. Gann taught that after any
stock experiences a large advance or large decline, it
requires time to tell when the next big move is going
to start, and traders who stare at the tape, day by
day, will get fooled many times. Therefore, Gann
said, a trader should wait until he gets a definite
indication before deciding that the big trend has
turned and a major move started. The larger the capital stock of the company, or the more shares outstanding, the longer it requires to complete accumulation or distribution. The length of time, as well as
the total number of points that a stock has moved
up or down from high or low levels, must be considered in judging whether accumulation or distribution
is taking place, according to Gann.

Gann also taught that the time factor was an important consideration when trying to anticipate a
stock's behavior. He wrote that when a stock uses
up several months' time either in accumulation or
distribution, it will require, then, several months for
the run between accumulation and distribution to
take place. "All of the stock is not sold on the first
rally, nor even on the second or third. Stock has to
be bought, and the market supported on the way
up, until it reaches a level where the supply is
greater than the demand and the insiders are willing
to sell out. Then it hesitates and moves up and
down over a narrow or wide range, according to
the kind of stock, until distribution is completed.

"The same occurs when a stock starts down. It requires a long time to convince people that after a stock has been selling at 140, it is going down to 100 points. Some people buy when it is down 10 points, others buy on 30, 40 and 50-point reactions, believing the stock cheap because they remember the price at which it formerly sold — 140, with the result that when it continues downward, they all get scared and all sell out, causing the last rapid decline which may be anywhere from 10 to 30 points."[8]

Gann concluded: "If people would only learn to watch and wait, they could make a lot more money, but they are in too big a hurry to get rich, and the result is they go broke. They buy or sell on hope, without a reason."[9] To help you avoid these and similar pitfalls we will next move on to a discussion of Gann's views on chart reading. As we alluded to earlier in this chapter, it was essential to his trading success.

Gann also taught that the time factor was an important consideration when trying to anticipate a stock's behavior. When a stock uses up several months' time either in accumulation or distribution, it will require, then, several months for the run between accumulation and distribution to take place.

NOTES

1 Gann, W.D., *Truth of the Stock Tape*, Lambert Gann Publishing, Pomeroy, Washington, 1923, pg 7.

2 Ibid., pg. 6

3 Ibid., pg. 6

4 Ibid., pg. 7

5 Ibid., pg. 67

6 Ibid., pg. 82

7 Ibid., pg. 12

8 Ibid., pg. 86

9 Ibid., pg. 86

CHAPTER 4

Gann's Chart-Reading Technique

G ann was a big believer in using financial charts to judge the soundness of common stocks and commodities. "All of the information that affects the future price of [stocks and commodities] is contained in its fluctuations and you need nothing more than its record of prices," he used to say. Most of his work was based around various ways of interpreting the chart, and without it, his forecasting success would have been largely impossible.

Gann's fundamental premise behind the use of charts in trying to predict price trends is the old maxim that "history repeats."

The fundamental premise behind the use of charts in trying to predict price trends is the old maxim that "history repeats." Gann was fond of quoting the passage of Ecclesiastes in the Bible, which says, "The thing that hath been, it is that which shall be; and that which is done, is that which shall be done; and there is no new thing under the sun."

"This shows that history is but a repetition of the past and that charts are the only guide we have of what stocks have done and by which we may determine what they will do," Gann would say. [1]

Along with the price indications provided by the chart, Gann always paid special attention to the trading volume behind the price movements. "The volume of sales on each individual stock shows the percentage that is being bought and sold. That is why the tape and price fluctuations tell the truth, provided one interprets the tape correctly."[2] Gann pointed out that a stock cannot be distributed or accumulated without a large volume of sales. Someone must buy and sell a large percent of the capital stock near the bottom or top in order to cause a big move in either direction. Therefore, Gann urged traders to study volume closely, along with the time required to sell a large amount of stock and the number of points which it moves up or down while the volume of sales is accumulating. "Study the volume of sales at each important bottom and top and consider the number of shares outstanding in each stock," was his frequent admonition. "This will help you to determine whether buying is better than selling, or not."[3]

One of Gann's rules concerning volume was that if a stock has a very large volume of sales in a day and has made a very narrow range in fluctuations, do not buy or sell until it shows a wider range of fluctuations, and go with the trend whichever way the move starts. Gann urged his students to keep up a daily, weekly, monthly and yearly chart showing the highs and lows for each respective time frame. By doing this, he said, a trader or investor can obtain an accurate picture of the overall position — strong or weak — of the stock he is following. "This is the proper way to read the stock tape," he said.

Gann provided the example of U.S. Steel — a popular stock in his day and one of his favorites to trade in — to illustrate one of his rules concerning volume. "Suppose U.S. Steel has advanced 20 or 30 points, and it reaches a level where there are 200,000 shares in one day, but the stock only gains one point. The next day there are 200,000 shares and it makes no gain. This is plain enough that at this point the supply of stock exceeds the demand, or at least that buyers are able to get all the stock they want without bidding prices up. In a case of this kind, the wise thing to do is to sell out, watch and wait. If all the stock at this level is absorbed after a reasonable length of time, and it moves up to new high prices, it will then, of course, indicate still higher.

"In a big bull market, when stocks reach the distributing zone, they will fluctuate over a wide range and the volume of sales will run several times the total outstanding capital stock. For instance: In the latter part of 1919 and spring of 1920, Baldwin Locomotive sales ran from 300,000 to 500,000 shares per week, while the stock was fluctuating between 130 and 156. This was when distribution was taking place, and the public was full of hope and buying regardless of price."

"After that, a long decline started and Baldwin reacted to 62³/₈ during the week ending June 25, 1921. It was down 93 points from the high of 1919. During the last week of the decline, it went down from 70 to 62³/₈ , over seven points, and the total sales for the week were less than 110,000, which showed that liquidation had about run its course and that there was very little stock pressing

Gann urged his students to keep up a daily, weekly, monthly and yearly chart showing the highs and lows for each respective time frame. By doing this, he said, a trader or investor can obtain an accurate picture of the overall position — strong or weak — of the stock he is following.

for sale. The amount of sales at this time, in one week, were about half of the capital stock and probably about as much as the floating supply, while when the stock was nearly 100 points higher, the capital stock was changing hands about twice each week."[4]

The normal pattern then ensued as Baldwin began to rally from the June 1921 lows of 62³/8 on light volume. This indicated that there were not many shares for sale and that the stock had passed from the weak hands to strong ones. Therefore it was very easy to rally this stock. The stock advanced to a high of 142 in October 1922. At this point another distribution phase took place. Observing many examples such as this reinforced Gann's view that volume was one of the key ingredients to trading success.

Gann taught that by studying past history and knowing that the future is but a repetition of the past, one can determine the cause according to the time and conditions.

Gann taught that by studying past history and knowing that the future is but a repetition of the past, one can determine the cause according to the time and conditions. "The average man's memory is too short," Gann wrote. "He only remembers what he wants to remember or what suits his hopes and fears. He depends too much on others and does not think for himself. Therefore, he should keep a record, graph or picture of past market movements to remind him that what has happened in the past can and will happen in the future, and should not allow his enthusiasm to get the better of his judgment and buy on hope, thinking that there will never be another panic."

Gann provided several useful rules for using chart analysis to determine when a bear market had ended. He taught that a bear campaign must run three to four sections before the bottom is reached. "Look over your charts and you will find that each group of stocks and each individual stock, when it starts on the down trend, runs out three to four sections. First, it has a sharp decline; then rallies and is distributed; then has another decline; hesitates, rallies and then has another decline; hesitates again and then has a final big break, or one we call the clean-out, when investors and everybody get scared and decide that stocks are never going up again and sell everything. When this final clean-out comes, that is the time to buy for the long pull for another bull campaign."

The Best Charts to Use

An extremely important distinction Gann made was in which kinds of charts to use. For instance, Gann did not believe in using space charts, also known as "point-and-figure" charts, because they do not contain the critical time element, instead displaying price only. The other type of chart that Gann said was most likely to fool traders, by producing false moves, is the daily bar chart. The weak point with these charts is the fact that they show the minor moves, which Gann likened to the ripples in the ocean caused by a pebble. They do not disturb or determine the big move or main trend. Most traders use this kind of chart.

Gann believed that the best charts to use are the weekly, monthly and yearly charts. Gann liked using longer-term charts because they show more time, and the more time a chart shows, the more reliable

Gann believed that the best charts to use are the weekly, monthly and yearly charts. Gann liked using longer-term charts because they show more time, and the more time a chart shows, the more reliable are its indications.

are its indications. "The weekly and daily high and low charts are valuable when the markets are very active and are good to use on very high-priced stocks at the time they are culminating or in the final grand rush, because the daily and weekly will show the first change in trend," he wrote. "They are better to use at the tops of fast moves than they are at the bottom. However, when markets have a quick, sharp, panicky decline, then the daily and weekly charts will help, but the best guides in long pull trading and determining the main trend are the yearly and monthly high and low charts."

Later in his life, Gann urged his students to also use quarterly charts in their attempts at determining market trends. In one of the last books he wrote, *How to Make Profits in Commodities* (1951) Gann had this to say about the quarterly chart:

"The more time period used in a chart, the more important it is for determining a change in trend. By a quarterly chart, or a seasonal chart, we mean a chart using the four time periods or seasons of the year. We use the first three months of the year — January, February, and March. Then we use the high and low prices of wheat, soybeans, or other commodities for these three months, the winter quarter. Next, we use April, May, and June to complete the spring quarter. After that, July, August, and September for the summer quarter. Last, October, November, and December for the fall quarter. This makes four periods, of three months each, in each year. Study a quarterly chart carefully, and you will see how these quarterly periods show when an important change in trend takes place. Observe how many times, after a prolonged advance or decline, the first time prices break the bottom of a previous quarter it indicates a change in trend, and a bear market starts. The first time the prices of one quarter exceed the high levels of the previous quarter, it nearly always indicates a change in trend, and a bull market follows. If you will study any quarterly chart carefully and note the position of wheat, or any other commodity, in connection with the monthly high and low chart, and the weekly high and low chart, you will find it very helpful in determining a change in the main trend. I advise keeping up a quarterly chart on each individual commodity that you trade in."[5]

Gann laid down several rules for studying the daily, weekly, and monthly charts and determining their respective positions. He advised watching the action of the daily moves in the first, second, third and fourth stage. If a stock begins an advance, then hesitates and begins a sideways or lateral movement and goes through resistance levels on the upside, he advised watching how it acts when it hesitates and stops the second, third and fourth times. When it reaches the third or fourth move up, he advised watching for a change in trend, as this represents the culmination period of the move. The same rule applies to the first, second and third moves on the weekly and monthly charts. It also applies to the major as well as the minor swings. According to Gann, when a market begins declining or an individual stock starts down, it usually makes two, three and four movements before it reaches final bottom.

According to Gann, when a market begins declining or an individual stock starts down, it usually makes two, three and four movements before it reaches final bottom. If the trend is going to reverse, it will only make the first and second decline and then turn up again. But after a prolonged decline and a fourth move down, Gann advised watching for a bottom to form and a change in trend.

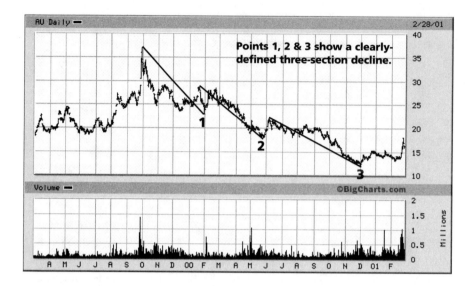

Points 1, 2 & 3 show a clearly-defined three-section decline.

FIGURE 4-1:
Two-year daily
chart of
Anglogold (AU)

If the trend is going to reverse, it will only make the first and second decline and then turn up again. But, after a prolonged decline and a fourth move down, Gann advised watching for a bottom to form and a change in trend.

Figure 4-1: Note the clearly-defined three-section decline in the above stock chart for Anglogold, from November 1999 through January 2001.

Different Time Frames

For daily trading or short-swing trading, Gann advised never buying or selling a stock until it has halted for two to three days at the bottom or top, which will show that buying or selling is strong enough to check the advance or decline. He advised buying or selling and placing a stop-loss order not more than 3 points above or below the extreme high or low point at which the stock halted.

This rule, however, should not be applied in panics. On the days of extreme fluctuations and large volume, it is not necessary to wait two or three days, because the market will have a sharp reverse move up or down. Therefore, Gann advised taking profits on the days of a fast advance and, when there are big, panicky declines, to cover shorts and wait to see what the market does the following days. He urged traders to judge each stock according to its position and not to expect it to follow the movement of its own group unless its graph shows that it is in position to do so.

Gann's time rule for judging the overall position of weekly charts involves waiting for a reaction of two to three weeks and then to buy. This applies to active stocks, as most of the active stocks will not react more than three to four weeks before the main trend is resumed. When in a bear market, reverse this rule; sell on rallies of two to three weeks. Gann instructed to always watch for a change in trend in the third week, up or down.

Gann's weekly rule for rapid advances and rapid declines is to watch for a culmination in the sixth or seventh week, up or down; then buy or sell after watching the daily high and low chart for the week that the stock reaches top or bottom, then place a stop-loss order above or below the resistance level.

His monthly time rule was based on the supposition that stocks that are in a strong position and show a pronounced upward trend will seldom ever react

Throughout his writings, Gann continually emphasized the importance of placing protective stops on all trades, reminding the reader that big losses are prevented this way and profits preserved.

into the second month. His rule was to buy and place a stop-loss order under the previous month's low level. Always watch the point at which advances start, whether from the lowest bottom or first, second, third, or fourth higher bottoms. These starting points are always buying points with a protective stop 3 points underneath. When a stock declines or advances after making top or bottom and the movement runs into the second month, the next important time to watch for a change in trend is the third or fourth month, according to Gann.

All of these rules work best in the stocks that are very active and are fluctuating on large volume of sales. Gann encouraged traders to study daily, weekly, and monthly high and low charts of the active high-priced stocks in order to learn how well his rules work.

Apart from studying price movements along different time frames, Gann also advised paying close attention to specific hours, days, and months of the year in order to determine potential turning points in stocks.

Apart from studying price movements along different time frames, Gann also advised paying close attention to specific hours, days, and months of the year in order to determine potential turning points in stocks. He observed that important changes in price often take place on Monday in the first hour of trade. "If a stock opens low on Monday and does not sell lower by 12 o'clock, it is a good sign," he said. The next important day of the week to watch for a change in trend, according to Gann, is Wednesday, especially Wednesday afternoon.

Gann also taught that it is very important to watch how stocks act during the first few days of the month. Important changes often occur between the first and third of each month, he noted. "One reason for this is that customers always receive their statements on the first of each month and know just how their accounts stand. They often sell out to secure profits or sell out because their accounts have been weakened by declines." The 10th of the month was also important for a change in trend for Gann. The 15th is also important but not as much as the 10th, he said. The 20th to 23rd is an important time to watch for a change in trend as well, since high or low prices are often reached around this time of the month.

"My experience has proven that the above dates are important and of value to any trader who will watch them, and will many times help in determining top or bottom," wrote Gann.

Gann also advised watching for annual and seasonal changes in stocks. "It is important to study past movements of stocks to see how much time is usually required to complete a movement," he wrote. "There are several sections to a major movement or swing. There are yearly and seasonal changes in all stocks, and you must watch for these seasonal changes. It is also important to watch for changes in trend every third, sixth, ninth and 12th month, but the most important time to watch for a major change in trend is at the end of each year. By this, I do not mean the calendar year. For example, if a stock makes bottom in the month of August, and the trend continues up; then the most important date would be the following August or one year later, when you should watch for at least a change in the minor trend, which might last one to three months or more.

It is important to study past movements of stocks to see how much time is usually required to complete a movement.

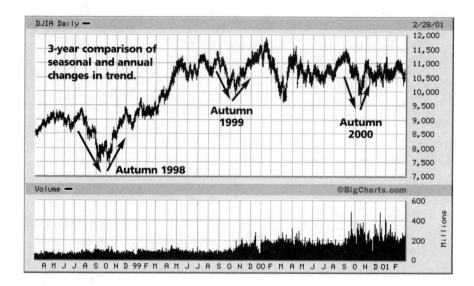

FIGURE 4-2:
Three-year daily
chart of the Dow
Jones Industrial
Average (DJIA).

Figure 4-2: Notice the seasonal tendency for the Dow Jones Industrial Average to decline into autumn, then reverse in the October-November time frame.

▲ ▲ ▲

In this chapter we have outlined how chart reading can be adapted to accurately predict and successfully trade during a wide variety of market conditions. Equally important in Gann's work was correctly identifying periods of accumulation and distribution. He said that, "The big profits are made in the runs between accumulation and distribution."[6] In the next chapter we will take a more complete look at the methods Gann used to recognize important patterns of accumulation and distribution that could help determine your next trading move.

NOTES

1 Gann, W.D., *Truth of the Stock Tape*, Lambert Gann Publishing, Pomeroy, Washington, 1923, pg. 52.

2 Ibid., pg. 2

3 Ibid., pg. 82

4 Ibid., pg. 53

5 Gann, W.D., *How to Make Profits in Commodities*, Lambert Gann Publishing, Pomeroy, Washington, 1951, pg 30.

CHAPTER 5

Identifying Accumulation and Distribution

To Gann, areas of congestion, that is, sideways movements on charts which fluctuate in a fairly narrow range over a considerable length of time, were extremely important for being able to locate areas of accumulation and distribution. More importantly, the path — whether upward or downward — that prices took after breaking out of these lateral zones usually determined whether the zone represented accumulation (buying) or distribution (selling). Therefore, by observing the path that prices take after breaking out of a trading range, a trader can profit by following the trend, expecting it to remain intact for a while. "After great activity and a long time in a narrow or wide range at top or bottom," he wrote, "a big move follows in which you can make profits rapidly." This technique of being able to interpret accumulation and distribution by the use of charts was the essence of Gann's "tape reading" success. To him chart areas showing either accumulation or distribution were the embodiment of supply and demand.

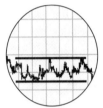

Congestion areas are sideways movements on charts which fluctuate in a fairly narrow range over a considerable length of time and are extremely important in identifying areas of accumulation and distribution.

Accumulation: A Foundation

The path—whether upward or downward—that prices take after breaking out of these lateral zones or areas of congestion, usually determines whether the zone represents accumulation (buying) or distribution (selling).

"Before any stock, or group of stocks, starts on a big advance or decline, a long period of time is required for preparation, or accumulation or distribution," wrote Gann in *Truth of the Stock Tape*. "It requires time to prepare and lay the foundation for a building. The larger the building, the more time required to construct the foundation. It is the same with stocks. The greater the advance or the decline, the more time required in preparing it."[1]

Gann provides us the example of his old favorite, U.S. Steel: "Take U.S. Steel, which was incorporated February 1901. It was a new stock and the largest corporation of its kind in the world at that time. Its common stock was all water, and as water seeks its level, Steel common with its five-million shares of water had to seek its level. It required many years to reach that level. The stock declined from 55 in 1901 down to 8³/₈ in 1904. When it reached the level of 12 it remained from December, 1903 to September, 1904 fluctuating between 12 and 8³/₈. Most of the time the fluctuations were between 9 and 10. It was at very low ebb, slow narrow fluctuations with very small volume of sales. This is where accumulation took place, which required about ten months and gave you ample time to watch it and see that it was receiving support. You did not have to be in a hurry about buying, as it was preparing for its long advance.

Accumulation (buying)

Distribution (selling)

"We will overlook the top at 94⁷/₈ in 1909. However, you can look it up for yourself and see that the entire capital stock changed hands several times between 88 and 94, and some days the trading in this stock alone ran over half a million shares, which, of course, showed that it was being distributed."[2]

Here again Gann emphasized the special importance of trading volume in deciding whether a certain level on a price chart represents accumulation or distribution. "The reaction or decline which must follow [accumulation or distribution] will be in proportion to the volume of sales and the heights to which stocks have risen. The volume of trading is just the same as a large volume of water. If it is two or three times greater than normal, it must spread over a larger area, break the dams and do great damage."[3]

He added, "The volume of sales always increases when stocks advance. This applies to days, weeks, months and years. When liquidation is going on and has about run its course, the volume decreases. The years of bear markets always show small volume and the years of bull markets always show very large volume. When a market is working lower, the volume of sales is very small in the last year of a bear campaign, which shows that liquidation has run its course."[4]

Gann concluded, "A study of the volume for each week, month, and year on the individual stocks will help you in determining the trend."[5]

The chart for BAP on the next page, Figure 5-1, shows distinctive reversals of trend whenever a conspicuous spike in trading volume appears. The trader must determine the overall trend and technical position of the market in order to ascertain whether the

Volume represents the number of shares traded

Gann emphasized the special importance of trading volume in deciding whether a certain level on a price chart represents accumulation or distribution. Conspicuous spikes in trading volume, usually are indicative of a reversal in trend — whether upward or downward.

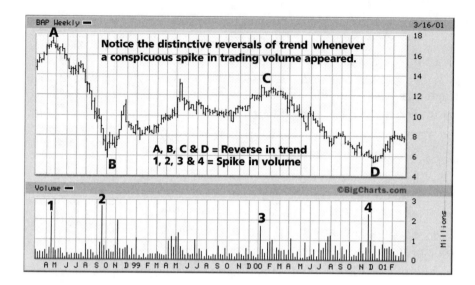

BAP Weekly ▬   3/16/01

Notice the distinctive reversals of trend whenever a conspicuous spike in trading volume appeared.

A

C

A, B, C & D = Reverse in trend
1, 2, 3 & 4 = Spike in volume

B

D

Volume ▬   ©BigCharts.com

1   2   3   4

A M J J A S O N D 99 F M A M J J A S O N D00 F M A M J J A S O N D 01 F

Millions

**FIGURE 5-1:
Three-year week-
ly chart of
Creditcorp (BAP)**

volume spikes represent a likely reversal upward or downward.

One of his favorite methods for doing this was to add up the total volume of sales that a stock makes in going from an extreme low to an extreme high. Gann shows us how:

"On December 22, 1928, the low on U.S. Steel was 149¾, and it worked higher all the time from this level until September 3, 1929, when it reached 261¾. The total sales during this period were 18,895,000 shares. The total outstanding shares of U.S. Steel are only a little over 8 million. Thus, in this advance, the total outstanding shares changed hands twice. From May 31, 1929, when the stock sold at 162½ the last time, being down 30 points from the high of March, it advanced to 261¾ on September 3, 1929, being up nearly 100 points. The total sales during this period were 7,615,100 shares, almost as much as the entire capital stock outstanding. Then, during the period from September 3, 1929, when the stock made a top at 261¾, to November 13, 1929, when it reached a low of 150, the total sales were 7,365,300 shares. Note how near these two total volumes of sales came to being equal. This was another good indication for bottom, when the number of shares on the decline equaled or nearly equaled the number of shares on the advance.

"If you will study the daily, weekly and monthly volume of sales on culminations of each different stock, you will find it very helpful in judging when it is in a strong or weak position."[6]

Gann believed that the best way to make money in the markets was to follow the trend, whether up or down, and to avoid trading against the trend at all times. One simple method for determining whether the trend is up or down is to note the overall trajectory of the priceline, especially the progressive tops and bottoms being made along the way. "Progressive" tops and bottoms was an operative term used by Gann to describe how far apart the tops and bottoms were spaced apart from each other. "As long as a stock makes higher bottoms and higher tops, the trend is up and it is safe to follow the advance," he wrote. "This rule applies to daily, weekly, monthly or yearly movements."[7] The exact opposite is true of bear markets—as long as a stock makes lower bottoms and lower tops, the trend is down and is therefore safe for following on the decline.

One simple method for determining whether the trend is up or down is to note the overall trajectory of the priceline, especially the progressive tops and bottoms being made along the way.

Swing Charts

This leads us to one of Gann's most important trading techniques for forecasting price movements and determining trends: the "swing" chart. Much has been written on this method over the years, and Gann himself provides us with considerable comment on the subject. He had various ways of constructing a swing chart, which is basically a chart in which extreme tops and bottoms of each time increment (whether a day, week, month, or year, depending upon the type of chart used) is connected with a line for every two or three period move in a single direction. Gann preferred the 3-increment swing method, though there is evidence that in his later years he reverted to a 2-increment swing rule.[8] However, since the great body of his writing on the subject deals with the 3-increment swing we will focus on that here.

The basis of Gann's use of the swing chart is summarized in his "Rule of Three," which he explains as follows:

"This is one of my discoveries of a method for making big profits in a short time trading in active, fast-moving stocks. I have made a lot of money with it, and some traders have paid me as much as $1,000 for this method. . . .

"The rule is this: A stock which shows strong up-trend will never close 3 consecutive days with losses. When it does close 3 consecutive days with losses, then it indicates that the trend has reversed, at least temporarily, and the longer a stock runs before

One of Gann's most important trading techniques for forecasting price movements and determining trends was the "swing" chart.

making 3 days' reactions, or closing 3 days at lower prices than the previous days, the surer indication it will be that the move is over. The same rule applies when a stock is declining. It will never close more than 2 days with gains or at higher prices. When it does close for 3 consecutive days with a gain, or a balance on the credit side, then it indicates that the trend has reversed, at least temporarily, and may mean a big move up. It makes no difference how high or low a stock goes during the market hours; the price at which is closes shows whether it has made a gain or loss over the previous day and whether it should be placed on the credit or debit side of your ledger. This is one of the most valuable rules for trading in high-priced active stocks. It will help you to get the benefit of the fast advances or declines and enable you to know when the minor trend is changing. Apply this same rule to the weekly and monthly high and low charts."[9]

An example of a Gann swing chart is provided in Figure 5-2 on the next page. Note carefully its construction. Gann's rule for determining the trend

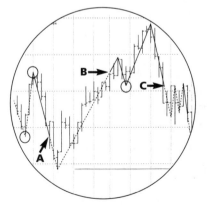

Notice how the trend lines change from solid (up trend) to dotted (down trend) at points A, B, and C. It is at these points that the trend line has penetrated a previous peak or valley (circled areas) formed by the price swing.

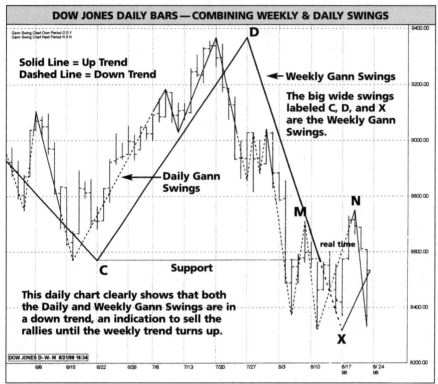

DOW JONES DAILY BARS — COMBINING WEEKLY & DAILY SWINGS

Gann Swing Chart Own Period O D Y
Gann Swing Chart Next Period N D N

Solid Line = Up Trend
Dashed Line = Down Trend

← Weekly Gann Swings

The big wide swings labeled C, D, and X are the Weekly Gann Swings.

←Daily Gann Swings

D

M

N

real time

C

Support

This daily chart clearly shows that both the Daily and Weekly Gann Swings are in a down trend, an indication to sell the rallies until the weekly trend turns up.

X

DOW JONES D- W- M 8/21/98 16:34

6/8   6/15   6/22   6/29   7/6   7/13   7/20   7/27   8/3   8/10   8/17   8/ 24
                                                                                          98   98

9400.00
9200.00
9000.00
8800.00
8600.00
8400.00
8200.00

FIBONACCI TRADER © Robert Krausz

FIGURE 5-2:
Dow Jones daily bars combining Daily and Weekly Gann Swings

based on the swing chart was that a price extreme (peak or valley), when penetrated, means the trend has turned down or up, depending on whether the price extreme was made in the ascending phase or descending phase. Gann also found that price objectives could be forecast by measuring the amplitude of the preceding swing—whether up or down—and adding this measurement (in terms of points) onto the beginning of the next swing. Often, the previous swing will forecast the amplitude of the forthcoming swing in both price and time.

The formula for constructing swing charts provided in the paragraphs on the previous pages, apply for daily, weekly, and monthly charts alike.

Gann's "Rule of Five"

Another important rule that Gann determined for judging whether accumulation or distribution was taking place was based on the number 5, which Gann taught was the "number of ascendancy." He observed that the fifth day, week, month or year of a market move—whether up or down—often was the culminating move before a reversal set in, and that it tended to be the most dynamic. He also applied this "rule of five" to judging whether accumulation (buying) or distribution (selling) was taking place in a given stock or commodity. For example, he taught that the sure sign of accumulation or distribution is a stock moving up or down many times over the same range, especially making moves of 5 points or more without getting above its high point, and at the same time not breaking under its resistance levels on the down side. Gann advised that when prices began fluctuating feverishly and rapidly as trading volume expands, then get out, watch and wait; that is, sell out your long positions and wait for the opportunity to sell short. "Never be in a hurry to get in again once you are out with a good profit," he warned.

Gann noted that wide fluctuations occur much more frequently at high levels than at low levels, mainly because distribution is taking place. "When stocks reach very low levels after a final drive, they slow

Another important rule that Gann determined for judging whether accumulation or distribution was taking place was based on the number 5.

He observed that the fifth day, week, month or year of a market move—whether up or down—often was the culminating move before a reversal set in, and that it tended to be the most dynamic.

down and often work for some time in a very narrow range while accumulation is taking place. Accumulation and distribution are exactly opposite. When the insiders want to sell stocks, they make all the noise possible and do everything to attract the attention of the public and create a large public buying power. When stocks decline to low levels and they want to accumulate a large line, they work just as quietly as possible. They use every means to disguise the fact that they are buying stocks, and do everything to discourage the outsiders from buying them."[10]

Gann taught that when stocks establish certain levels of accumulation or distribution over a long number of months or years and then cross them, it is almost a sure sign that they are going to new high or low levels before they meet with resistance again.

Gann taught that when stocks establish certain levels of accumulation or distribution over a long number of months or years and then cross them, it is almost a sure sign that they are going to new high or low levels before they meet with resistance again. "As a rule," he wrote, "it is always safe to buy or sell a stock around old bottoms or tops with a stop-loss order three points above or below previous high or low prices." He added that when stocks advance near old high levels and remain a long time and fail to go through, distribution is taking place, and as soon as they break out of the distributing zone, they should be sold short.

"When a market starts to advance," wrote Gann, "it continues upward until it reaches a level where supply and demand are about equal and prices come to a standstill. Then supply increases until it exceeds demand, and prices start to decline.

"In a long decline or a long advance, a level is reached where the supply is absorbed and prices go on to the next level, where they meet another large supply and absorb it, and finally to a level where the supply is so much greater than the demand that distribution takes place and prices start on a long trend down. This is why many weeks and sometimes several months are required at bottom or top to complete accumulation or distribution before a big move starts.

"People who buy or sell the first or second time that the market halts after the trend turns, invariably lose money because it is simply a halting period to absorb offerings or to supply a demand at that level, after which the main trend moves on to the next level. For this reason, it does not pay to buck the trend — always go with it. If you trade against the trend for a quick turn and get a small profit, accept it; do not expect too much. At the same time, protect your trade with a stop-loss order and do not let it run against you when you are bucking the trend."[11]

▲ ▲ ▲

Gann's views on accumulation and distribution are clearly explained in his many writings as are his trading rules. Applying his methods and utilizing his swing charts over the long run can significantly improve one's percentage of winning trades. In our next chapter we will discuss his Law of Vibration, which many market historians felt was left purposefully vague and remains a topic of discussion even to this day.

NOTES

1 Gann, W.D., *Truth of the Stock Tape*, Lambert Gann Publishing, Pomeroy, Washington, 1923, pg. 103.

2 Ibid., pg. 103

3 Ibid., pg. 104

4 Ibid., pg. 74

5 Ibid., pg. 73

6 Ibid., pg. 165

7 Ibid., pg. 109

8 In his book, *A W.D. Gann Treasure Discovered: Simple Trading Plans for Stocks & Commodities* (Geometric Traders Institute, Ft. Lauderdale, Fla., 1998), Robert Krausz unveils a long-lost trading course written by Gann himself to one of his students in which he altered his "rule of three" swing trading principle, advising instead a two-day (or two-week, -month-, etc., depending on chart time frame) swing rule.

9 Gann, W.D., *Truth of the Stock Tape*, Lambert Gann Publishing, Pomeroy, Washington, 1923, pg. 49.

10 Ibid., pg. 61

11 Ibid., pg. 62

CHAPTER 6

The Law of Vibration

G ann was as much a devoted student of natural philosophy as he was of the financial markets. He spent years studying the laws of physics and applied that learning to his market forecasting methods.

One of the important observations he made in his study of science he called the "Law of Vibration." Gann claimed that this scientific law was an essential feature of all living things and that it governed the movement of all physical bodies, including planetary bodies. Humans, animals, insects and planets all shared this common feature of the Law of Vibration.

What exactly this "Law of Vibration" was, Gann never made clear. His writings make frequent reference to it and he always claimed that he could make huge profits in the stock and commodity markets by applying it to his chart-reading technique, but he never gave specific guidelines for its application. After carefully reading through Gann's works, however, one can gain a fair comprehension of what he was referring to.

Gann claimed that this scientific law was an essential feature of all living things and that it governed the movement of all physical bodies, including planetary bodies. Humans, animals, insects and planets all shared this common feature of the Law of Vibration.

It is my view that the Law of Vibration is a method for isolating chart congestion zones and measuring the upside or downside objective of the priceline once it has broken out of that zone. Apparently, Gann saw in these consolidations, or congestion zones (i.e., lateral trading channels), not merely zigzags on a chart but something far deeper in meaning. When prices behave in this manner, Gann saw them as resting from their previous movement and building up energy for their next big move. Gann even had a way of measuring the size of the anticipated move. By subtracting the extreme low of the trading range in which the consolidation occurred from the extreme high end of the range, then multiplying that number by 3 and 5 (300%-500%) Gann was able to forecast approximately how high (or how low) prices would move once they broke out of the zone of consolidation. He observed that it was common for prices to have rapid moves of 300%-500% after a prolonged sideways consolidation.

When the priceline on the chart "coils" or fluctuates rapidly in a narrow, lateral range it is actually building up energy for its next big move. This Gann discovered from his observations of the laws of nature, and science today would classify this under the explanations provided by vibratory physics. This rule works extremely well in any market and across many different time frames, whether yearly, monthly, weekly, daily, or intraday. Notice the chart example provided on the next page.

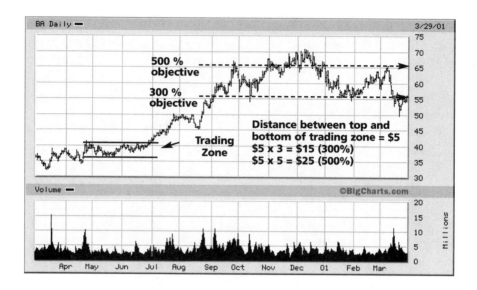

BA Daily ▬   3/29/01

500 % objective

300 % objective

Trading Zone

Distance between top and bottom of trading zone = $5
$5 x 3 = $15 (300%)
$5 x 5 = $25 (500%)

Volume ▬   ©BigCharts.com

Apr May Jun Jul Aug Sep Oct Nov Dec 01 Feb Mar

Millions

Figure 6-1. Boeing (BA)

FIGURE 6-1:
Two-year daily
chart of Boeing
(BA)

In Figure 6-1, Boeing's daily chart shows a trading zone between roughly the $36 and the $41 level, a distance of $5 from top to bottom. Multiplying $5 by 3 (to yield the 300% breakout objective) yields $15. Adding $15 to the top of the trading range at approximately $41 yields $56, an objective that was quickly reached once prices broke out of the range. Multiplying $5 by 5 (to get the 500% breakout objective) yields $25. By adding $25 to the top of the trading range of $41, the 500% breakout objective of $66 was reached three months later.

As this chart illustrates, this application of Gann's Law of Vibration, though not used to predict the *direction* of price movements, can be used as an accurate tool to forecast the *amplitude* of the move once it gets underway. The price targets that result from this analysis can make one's trading plan more effective. Let's now take a look at how Gann's chart-reading methodology applies in today's markets.

CHAPTER 7

Gann Analysis & Today's Markets

By now we have established Gann's most important rules for forecasting price movements and trading with safety and accuracy. You may be wondering if the methods Gann used 80 years ago are still valid today. Since a picture is worth a thousand words, let's apply Gann's chart-reading techniques to several of today's actively traded stocks and commodities in order to prove the merit of these rules.

Figure 7-1.   Intel Corp (INTC)

Crossing an old top was viewed by Gann as a sign of strength and therefore a buy signal. Here, Intel

A clear-cut buy signal is generated at the point when the price-line crosses above the previous top. A sell signal is generated at the point when the price falls below the base of support or previous bottom.

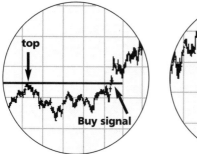
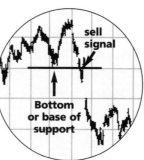

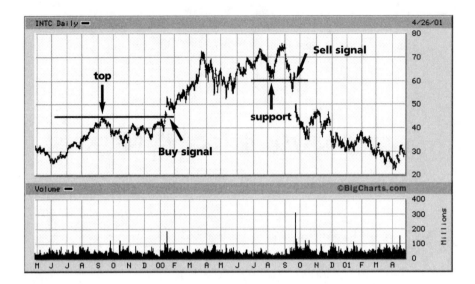

FIGURE 7-1:
Two-year chart of
Intel Corp (INTC)

Corp's (INTC) chart flashes a clear-cut buy signal in January 2000 when its priceline crosses above the previous top set in September the previous year. INTC continued the impressive run-up into August 2000 before reversing sharply to the downside. The violation of support at $60 was a reason to go short as INTC eventually dropped well below the $20 level.

Figure 7-2. Johnson & Johnson (JNJ)

To Gann, special consideration was always given to prolonged sideways movements on the chart, known as "consolidation" moves. During these phases of low volatility and a lack of a clearly defined trend, either accumulation (buying) or distribution (selling) is taking place. Rather than try to predict which way prices would move after the consolidation was completed, Gann taught that a trader should wait for the priceline itself to declare its intent, then follow it. A prime example of this favored Gann technique is found in the chart of Johnson & Johnson (JNJ). Note the protracted sideways trading range that developed between April 1999 and January 2000. Early in 2000 the priceline dropped beneath the floor of this range, indicating that distribution had been underway and that a downtrend was beginning. The trader should have sold short at this point. The declining trend continued until April before reversing. After a spike bottom, or "V-reversal" in April, the trader should have covered his short position and gone long. At the former trading range of $89-$106, Johnson & Johnson met with resistance once again. The trader should await a firm signal before initiating a trading position in JNJ.

**FIGURE 7-2:
Two-year chart
of Johnson &
Johnson (JNJ)**

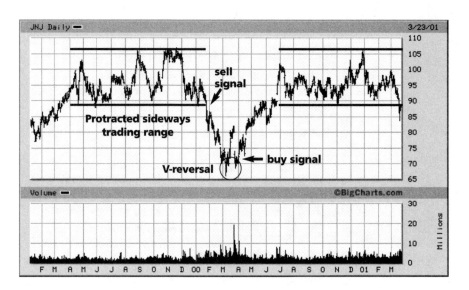

FIGURE 7-3:
One-year daily
chart of Boeing
(BA)

Figure 7-3. Boeing (BA)

Boeing is a good example of a short-sale candidate based on Gann's principle of waiting for the market to signal its intent, then following that signal. Boeing entered a sideways consolidation between November 2000 and December 2000 before breaking below the floor of its trading range at $62. The astute trader would have sold short from here awaiting the decline that was sure to follow. After another brief consolidation in February, Boeing did eventually decline to even lower levels.

A downward path of the price after breaking out of a lateral or sideways consolidation, represents distribution or selling.

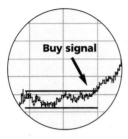

An upward path of the price after breaking out of a lateral or sideways consolidation, represents accumulation or buying.

Figure 7-4. Aviall Inc. (AVL)

The chart for AVL shows a defined trading range between $7-$9.75 between November 1999 and April 2000. When the floor of this range was broken, the trader should have followed the lead and sold short. After yet another lengthy period of consolidation, AVL broken out again of its trading range (between $4.50-$7) in January, this time to the upside. Note the large increase in volume on the breakout. The trader would have been safe in assuming an upward trend would follow.

FIGURE 7-4. One-year daily chart of Aviall Inc. (AVL)

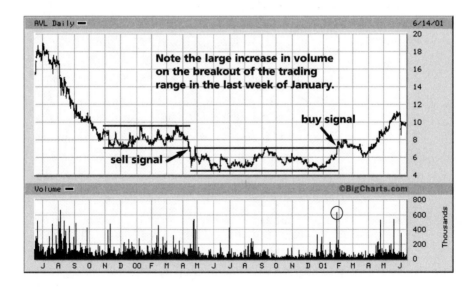

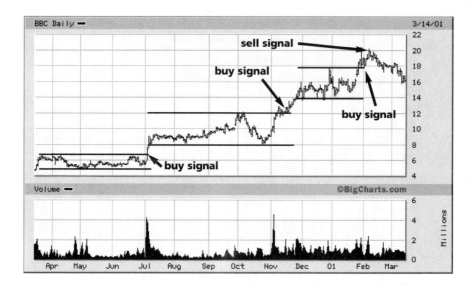

FIGURE 7-5:
One-year daily
chart of Bergen
Brunswig Corp.
(BBC)

Figure 7-5. Bergen Brunswig Corp. (BBC)

In the chart of Bergen Brunswig Corp. (BBC) we find three examples of how Gann's trading rules can be applied in rapid succession. Notice the three lateral ranges that developed between the $5-$6.50 level in April and July; the $8-$12 level in July and November; and the $14-$18 level in December 2000/January 2001. When the priceline broke above these ranges it was time to go long with BBC. Shortly after the third rapid succession, BBC met with resistance (i.e., selling pressure) at the $20 level. Gann taught that a trader should always watch round, whole numbers like 20, since many traders like to sell around these levels for psychological reasons. Sure enough, when the $20 level was approached, trading volume increased and the uptrend stalled out—an indication that BBC was meeting with heavy selling. The trader should have sold out his line of BBC at that time and awaited for the market to signal its next move.

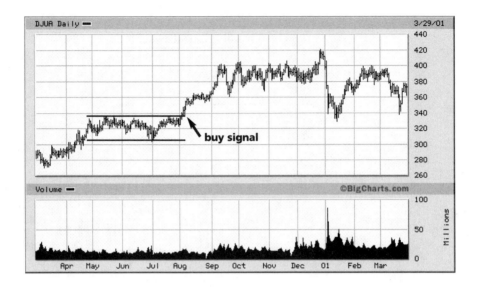

Figure 7-6. Dow Jones Utilities Average (DJUA)

**FIGURE 7-6:
Daily one-year
bar chart of Dow
Jones Utilities
Average (DJUA)**

Gann's chart reading technique works as well with major stock market indexes as it does with individual stocks. Notice the three-month lateral trading range that developed in the Dow Jones Utilities Average between the last week in April and the end of July 2000. When the top of this range was penetrated in August, the trader got his signal to buy utility stocks (or mutual funds indexed off the Dow Jones Utilities Average). A large rise of the priceline followed.

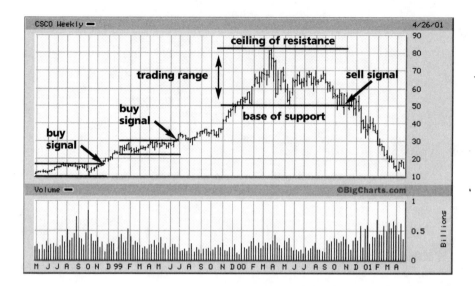

FIGURE 7-7:
Weekly three-
year chart of
Cisco Systems
(CSCO)

Figure 7-7. Cisco Systems (CSCO)

Cisco Systems (CSCO) weekly chart covers almost three years of trading and gives you a different perspective. It also is a good example of accumulation between $10.25 and $17.50 from May 1998 to the breakout in November of 1999. Then Cisco formed another trading range between $22.50 and $30.50 from January to June of 1999 before starting its surge to the eventual highs above $80.

Between February and October 2000, Cisco Systems showed a trading range between the $50 and $80 levels. The floor of this range was decisively broken in early October, at which time the trader should have sold short. CSCO eventually dropped below the $15 level.

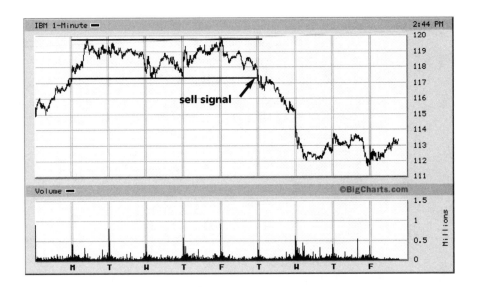

Figure 7-8. IBM

**FIGURE 7-8:
Intra-day chart
of IBM**

Gann's method of analyzing charts works equally
well with intra-day charts as it does with other time
frames. In the 1-minute intra-day chart for IBM
(spanning a period of 10 days), notice the trading
range that developed between $117.25 and
$119.75. When prices broke below the bottom of
this range, it was a signal for day traders to sell
short IBM in anticipation of a decline to $112 based
on the price objective rule. IBM did in fact fall to this
level over a two-day period.

This series of charts illustrates that not only do
Gann's methods work in today's markets, just like
they did 80 years ago, but hopefully encourage you
to look at charts in a different way. Though Gann is
very well known for uncanny predictions for the
stock market, he is equally legendary for his trading
and analysis of the commodity markets. He pub-

lished individual annual forecasts for the grains, cotton, coffee and sugar markets for which he charged the then exorbitant price of $100 annually, per market! In the next chapter we will review some of the methods that Gann used in the commodity markets.

CHAPTER 8

The W.D. Gann Method of Commodity Trading

"The commodity market," wrote Gann in his book, *How to Make Profits in Commodities*, "offers good opportunities every year for making profits both as an investment and as a speculative proposition. Trading in future options is just as legitimate as buying and selling stocks. It is not necessary to buy the spot cotton outright, carry it into the warehouses, pay insurance and storage, for if [for example] spot cotton is going up or down, future options will fluctuate more than the cash article, and there is no expense in carrying futures outside of the margin requirements."[1]

He continues, "The course of [commodity] prices is based on supply and demand, and it is much easier to form a correct judgment on the commodities market than it is on the stock market, on account of there being so many stocks and different groups of stocks which cause a mixed trend, some stocks declining while others advance. With commodities it is different. If one option [in a given commodity] goes up, they all go up. You might be right on a

"The course of [commodity] prices is based on supply and demand, and it is much easier to form a correct judgment on the commodities market than it is on the stock market. . . . "

certain group of stocks and yet pick the laggard to buy, and not make any money; but with commodities you could not miss it; if you were right on the trend you would make money. A man who trades in commodities with the proper capital and uses stop-loss orders to protect his capital and also to protect his profits will be able to make more money than he will trading in stocks, especially when [certain commodities] are active."[2]

Gann's rules for trading the commodities markets were simple and can be applied to any tradable commodity:

1. When you have nothing else to hold on for but hope, get out quick.

2. Never trade without a reason.

3. The time to hold on is when the market is going in your favor and not against you.

4. Cut short your losses and let your profits run.

5. Profits must be followed up with a stop-loss order, and your capital should always be protected by one.

Gann urged the commodity trader to learn to discount reports which come from analysts and brokerage offices. "They are honest," he wrote, "but they have commodities to sell and are always hoping for higher prices. They go to the extreme either way. If crops are bad, they exaggerate the damage. If crops are good, they are likely to become too hopeful and exaggerate the good condition...you must discount their reports and opinions."[3]

A man who trades in commodities with the proper capital and uses stop-loss orders to protect his capital and also to protect his profits will be able to make more money than he will trading in stocks, especially when [certain commodities] are active.

The importance of the "tape," i.e., the reading of price and volume fluctuations in the market, cannot be overlooked, according to Gann. "The tape tells you the consensus of opinion and reveals the predominance of the opposing forces and shows the trend according to supply and demand. Ignore the news, reports, opinions and views of everyone if it disagrees with what the chart and tape shows, for supply and demand must govern in the end, and if the selling power is greater than the buying, prices will decline, regardless of bad news or anything else. On the other hand, if the demand, or buying power, exceeds the selling, prices will advance regardless of good news. Of course, the general trend of the market does not continue for long contrary to natural conditions, but supply and demand govern the prices and the market discounts future events. Therefore, before you act too strongly on any good or bad news, be sure that your chart, which is but the reading of the tape and the correct interpretation of it, confirms the news and shows that it is yet to be discounted."[4]

Gann warned vigorously against the dangers of overtrading. He often claimed that overtrading was the cause of more profit losses on LaSalle Street (or Wall Street for that matter) than any other single factor.

Gann warned vigorously against the dangers of overtrading. He often claimed that overtrading was the cause of more profit losses on LaSalle Street (or Wall Street for that matter) than any other single factor. "Do not try to trade too often," Gann warned. "Jumping in and out of the market confuses you; the more trades you make the more chances you have for getting it wrong, and increasing the percentage against you. You can always make profits if you wait for the opportunities. If you make two or three consecutive trades and they go against you, and you have to take losses, better quit for a while and look on. Wait until your judgment gets clear, and the market shows a definite trend. You can always form a better judgment when you are out of the market than when you are in it, because you are not influenced by your hopes and fears."

According to Gann, one of the most important things that traders overlook is the amount of capital required to make a success trading in commodities. "A man should go into the commodities market the same as he goes into any other business — to make a success and not a gambling proposition," he wrote. "If you make speculation or investment a business, you probably will be able to accumulate a fortune over a number of years, but if you go into it to gamble and expect to make it all on one deal, you will lose all your money and have nothing left but hope." Gann advocated trading with no more than 10% of one's discretionary, or surplus, capital. "This money," he wrote, "is not to be used to put up on the [contract] and hold if it starts going against you. It is for the purpose of paying several small losses and still have capital enough left to continue to trade until you hit it right and begin to make big profits."[5]

As always, Gann advised commodity traders to use stop-loss orders when executing a trade, and to follow up profits by raising or lower stops (according to whether the trader is long or short a given contract). Gann further advised that once your mind is made up and you have placed your stop-loss order, do not cancel it or change it to where you have a greater loss if it is caught. "In 99 cases out of 100, you will be wrong when you place yourself in a position to take a greater loss than you first decided on. It may be well enough some times to cancel orders for taking profits if the market is going your way, but never cancel an order to stop a loss. The sooner a loss is stopped the better both for your capital and for your judgment. As long as you stay in the market and a trade goes against you, your judgment gets worse all the time; in fact, you have no judgment. It is simply a big hope that the market will turn and go your way."[6]

Another technique Gann used to rapidly multiply commodity-trading profits was one he called "pyramiding." This is performed most successfully in swift-moving markets. As a rule, Gann advised adding to one's trading position when the market moves in your favor by 10-20 percent. Each new position should be followed up by adjusting your stop-loss order so that it continually rises with, but stays beneath, the market. That way, should the market suddenly reverse, all of your profits will not be wiped out.

A technique Gann used to rapidly multiply commodity-trading profits was one he called "pyramiding."

Gann warned against the option trading strategy known as the "straddle," or "strangle" trade, where two options — one put and one call — are simultaneously purchased in the hope that one or the other will show a profit, and that further, the profit from the one will exceed the loss from the other. This strategy, of course, violates Gann's fundamental tenet of trading on hope rather than on the tape and chart indications. Wrote Gann, "Many traders get the idea that they can sell one option and buy another, thereby making a straddle which will work closer together and show them a profit. In nine cases out of ten, it works exactly opposite, and instead of a profit the result is a big loss. If you cannot form a judgment of the trend of the market, then do not try to play both sides at the same time. Something always happens to upset all calculations when traders figure out a dead sure cinch on a straddle. As a trader once said to me, 'My broker recommended something safe and sure — a good straddle — and I got on for a joy ride and the straddle tore both my legs off.' This is the way most straddles work out.

"Another great mistake that traders make is that when they buy one option and it starts to go against them, they refuse to see that they are wrong and accept a loss, but sell another option to hedge. Then they are both long and short of the market, and they have to make two guesses as to where they will get out right. It cannot be done. They invariably close the trade that shows a profit and hold the one that shows a loss. In this way, they undo the wrong side of the hedge. A man cannot have a clear judgment trying to play two sides of the market at the same time. It is bad enough playing one side. Therefore, keep out of hedges and straddles; try to determine the trend and follow it."[7]

The commodities market, like any market, is governed by the forces of supply and demand, which are judged by price and volume indications on the tape. Gann often stated that the only difference between reading the tape on a given commodity and reading it on stocks is that the commodity tape does not show the number of contracts traded in on each sale. This makes it a little difficult at times to determine the trend, but while one does not know the amount of trading that is going on, the fluctuations on the tape show very plainly whether the volume is heavy or light, according to Gann. "The market does not stand still on large buying or selling," he wrote. "It moves one way or the other. Therefore the activity tells us whether or not there is big business going on. When fluctuations are very narrow and the market is dull and inactive, it shows that the buying and selling is reduced to a small scale, and no big move is indicated. Therefore, the only thing to do is to watch and wait until you see activity start, and then go with it."[8]

Gann also provided some good advice for trading options on commodity futures: "It always pays to trade in the active options, and not trade when they get too close to maturity. There is no use taking chances on wild fluctuations and bad executions when you get near delivery dates. Trade in the next option where you can get good executions."

In regard to the commodities tape, Gann's advice was the same as it was with stocks — don't watch it too closely; instead, he advised keeping up a chart and reading the tape based on the high and low indications of the chart on all time frames — daily, weekly, monthly and yearly. In this way, a trader can best judge the short-term, intermediate-term and long-term trends influencing price movements in any market. Spotting those changes in trend is the topic of our next chapter.

In regard to the commodities tape, Gann's advice was the same as it was with stocks — don't watch it too closely; instead, he advised keeping up a chart and reading the tape based on the high and low indications of the chart on all time frames — daily, weekly, monthly and yearly.

NOTES

1 Gann, W.D., *How to Make Profits in Commodities*, Lambert Gann Publishing, Pomeroy, Washington, 1951, pg. 1.

2 Ibid., pg. 2

3 Ibid., pg. 15

4 Ibid., pg. 5

5 Ibid., pg. 4

6 Ibid., pg. 13

7 Ibid., pg. 18

8 Ibid., pg. 23

CHAPTER 9

Rules for Determining a Change in Trend

W.D. Gann was a master at reading the charts and the tape and was an expert stock and commodities trader as well. He shared much of this wisdom through his many writings on the subject of trading technique, including some of his trading secrets.

One of the methods Gann relied on most successfully for forecasting future price movements and profiting from the market, was being able to judge areas of accumulation and distribution on the charts.

One of the methods he relied on most successfully for forecasting future price movements and profiting from the market, was being able to judge areas of accumulation and distribution on the charts. To him, these were visible areas of buying and selling, and by following the direction the priceline took after breaking out of these trading ranges, he made enormous profits. He wrote several rules for determining when a trend begins and ends in the cotton market, many of which we will share here.

Gann wrote that when the market is fluctuating in a very narrow range, the cotton trader should keep up a chart of every 10-point move made during the day. "In this way," he wrote, "you will be able to see whether accumulation or distribution is taking place, and discern where resistance levels are formed. When it breaks out into new territory you can then follow the trend. In very active markets, when prices are high and range wide, fluctuations of 10 points mean very little, and you should keep a chart of every move of 30 to 40 points made during the day. In this way you will be able to locate the resistance levels and tell when it breaks out of the zone of accumulation or distribution."[1]

He wrote further, "You should always keep a monthly, weekly, and daily high and low chart on the active options you are trading in. It will only require fifteen to twenty minutes each day to do this and you will be well repaid for your trouble. The value of charts is to determine where support is given and where it is withdrawn; also where resistance is met on an advance and where it is overcome, thus enabling you to buy and sell and place a stop-loss order as close as possible for your protection."[2]

IBM Daily, Weekly, and Monthly Bar Charts

The three chart examples — daily, weekly, and monthly — for IBM on the opposite page, show differences across the various time frames. Notice on IBM's daily chart, Figure 9-1, the drop to the $80 level reflects technical weakness; however, IBM's weekly chart, Figure 9-2, shows strong support at this level in early 1999. On the monthly chart, Figure 9-3, the drop to $80 after rising from $13 to $135 does not seem too severe. Longer-term charts help the trader put things in perspective with respect to the overall technical position of a stock or commodity.

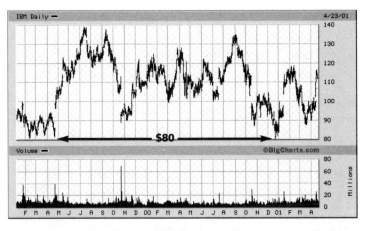

**FIGURE 9-1:
IBM Daily**

**FIGURE 9-2:
IBM Weekly**

**FIGURE 9-3:
IBM
Monthly**

Continuing, he writes, "After violent fluctuations up or down, the market nearly always comes to a standstill before the next move starts. Buying and selling becomes about equal and the market narrows down, then activity starts one way or the other and you should go with it. Of course, there are bound to be false moves at times. After accumulation is shown some news may develop which will cause a sharp drive down, followed by a quick rebound. Then if prices go above the levels previously established, you can consider that the move has reversed and that prices will continue upward."[3]

Gann noted that often, when the first top is made, a lot of profit taking will be encountered and a short interest will be built up. Something often will occur of a favorable nature to scare the shorts into covering, forcing prices to a slightly higher level, which weakens the technical position. Then a quick decline develops, and if previous low levels are broken and the market is very active on the decline, it will be an indication that the trend has again turned down, according to Gann.

"Do not try to trade every day," he advised. "Watch and wait for opportunities and once you see you are in right with the trend of the market, follow it up or down until you see a sign that the trend has reversed. Do not close your trade just because you have a profit, but always be convinced by the position of the chart and the general condition, that the trend has changed. Never buy after a lot of very bullish news comes out, nor sell after an extremely bearish report. Both good and bad news is nearly

> **Gann advised "Do not try to trade every day, watch and wait for opportunities and once you see you are in right with the trend of the market, follow it up or down until you see a sign that the trend has reversed.**

always discounted. Of course, consider whether the trend is up or down when good or bad news is made known."[4]

He advises further, "Remember [prices] can always go higher if conditions are right. [Do not] buy just because [prices are] . . . at low level[s], as [they] can always go lower. Never buck the trend, and do not try to guess the top or bottom. Wait until the chart shows you that the trend has turned. You can always make plenty of money buying or selling after the trend is well defined. The man who is in too big a hurry will lose money and miss opportunities just as often as the man who is too slow to act."[5]

"Follow the tape and the charts," concludes Gann, "for they will point to the correct course of prices according to the natural law of supply and demand."[6] Gann Angles can be used to quickly determine whether supply or demand is the dominating factor in a given market. They are possibly the most well known of Gann's technical tools and represent a significant contribution to the field of technical analysis. They are introduced in the next chapter.

NOTES

1 Gann, W.D., *Truth of the Stock Tape*, Lambert Gann
  Publishing, Pomeroy, Washington, 1923, pg. 165.

2 Ibid., pg. 165

3 Ibid., pg. 165

4 Ibid., pg. 166

5 Ibid., pg. 166

6 Ibid., pg. 169

CHAPTER 10

Gann Angles

Once the basic concepts of trend line support and resistance have been mastered, we can now proceed to a more advanced concept that allows for greater accuracy in market forecasting using charts. Employing a little-known technique developed by W.D. Gann, a trader can derive maximum leverage in negotiating the markets.

Gann was a master geometer as well as a master market technician. He saw many parallels between the concepts of geometry and the patterns in the market. He developed several ideas based on Greek geometry that he implemented in his trading system, ideas which proved highly accurate and which can be used in almost any market, including cotton. Known as "Gann Angles," this technique uses several degrees of trend lines to determine the overall position of the market, whether strong or weak.

All of Gann's techniques require that equal time and price intervals be used on the charts, so that a rise/run of 1 x 1 will always equal a 45 degree angle.[1] He believed that the ideal balance between time and price exists when prices rise or fall at a 45

The technique known as "Gann Angles," uses several degrees of trend lines to determine the overall position of the market, whether strong or weak.

degree angle relative to the time axis. This is also called a 1 x 1 angle (i.e., prices rise on price unit for each time unit).[2]

In his book, *Technical Analysis From A to Z*, Steven Achelis explains the concept of Gann Angles as follows: "Gann Angles are drawn between a significant bottom and top (or vice versa) at various angles. Deemed the most important by Gann, the 1 x 1 trend line signifies a bull market if prices are above the trend line or a bear market if below. Gann felt that a 1 x 1 trend line provides major support during an uptrend, and when the trend line is broken, it signifies a major reversal in the trend. Gann identified nine significant angles, with the 1 x 1 being the most important:

1 x 8 = 82.5 degrees
1 x 4 = 75 degrees
1 x 3 = 71.25 degrees
1 x 2 = 63.75 degrees
1 x 1 = 45 degrees
2 x 1 = 26.25 degrees
3 x 1 = 18.75 degrees
4 x 1 = 15 degrees
8 x 1 = 7.5 degrees

"Gann observed that each of the angles can provide support and resistance depending on the trend. For example, during an uptrend the 1 x 1 angle tends to provide major support. A major reversal is signified when prices fall below the 1 x 1 angled trend line. According to Gann, prices should then be expected to fall to the next trend line (i.e., the 2 x 1 angle). In other words, as one angle is penetrated, expect prices to move and consolidate at the next angle."[3]

> **The 1 x 1 trend line, deemed the most important by Gann, signifies a bull market if prices are above the trend line or a bear market if below. Gann felt that a 1 x 1 trend line provides major support during an uptrend, and when the trend line is broken, it signifies a major reversal in the trend.**

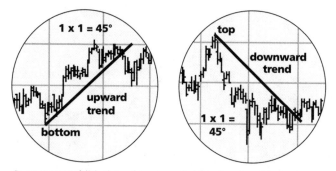

Once you establish the reference point for drawing the angle line—either a significant top (downtrend) or bottom (uptrend), you would then use a protractor to measure the various degrees. In an uptrend, the angle would be drawn upward from the bottom; in a downtrend, downward from the top.

Gann Angles are drawn by locating a significant top or bottom and using that as the reference point for drawing the angle line. From this top or bottom, draw a horizontal line outward and use a protractor to measure the various degrees, keeping in mind that the 45 degree line will be most important. Once you have isolated these degrees, use a ruler to draw the trend lines from the reference point outward. It will be noted that smaller degree of trend line, the less likely it is to have any significance. It has been our observation that when prices have broken below a 35 degree trend line, the entire move is in jeopardy of being reversed (even though Gann did not refer to a 35 degree trend line in his writings). The angles between 35 degrees and 45 degrees are always the most important ones, whether in an upward trend or downward trend.

Note the use of Gann Angles in the charts that follow on pages 93 and 94.

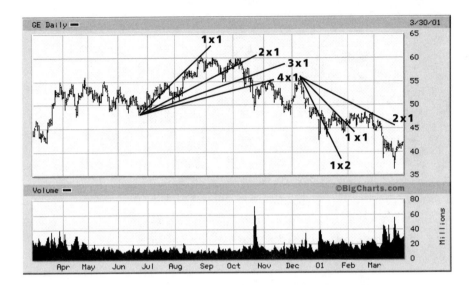

FIGURE 10-1: One-year daily chart of General Electric (GE)

Figure 10-1. General Electric (GE)

General Electric's chart shows four Gann Angle trend lines between June and October of 2000. Note the bullish 2 X 1 angle that was first penetrated in September, then decisively broken in October as were both the 3 X 1 and 4 x1. Each successive Gann Angle trend line was of a lower degree, hence, less bullish than the previous one. After the 4 X 1 angle was broken in October, a new series of downward-sloping Gann Angles developed in December: first the 1 X 2 angle, followed by the 1 X 1, and then the 2 x 1 angle. The steeper the angle in the declining phase, the more bearish the technical position of the market. Note that the 2 x 1 angle was tested in February before the stock plunged once more.

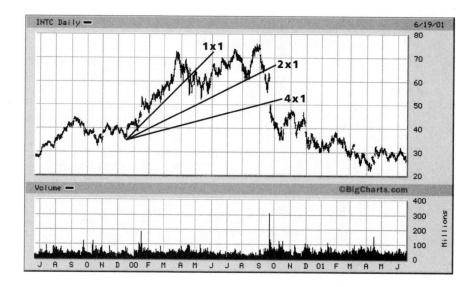

Figure 10-2. Intel (INTC)

Note the three clearly-defined series of Gann Angles in the chart for Intel. After the bullish 1 X 1 angle was broken in April 2000, it gave warning that the stock was losing upside momentum. This was confirmed when the 2 X 1 angle was broken in September. An extremely shallow 4 X 1 angle was broken later in the month, warning of much lower levels ahead.

Gann Angles are helpful tools to use when used in conjunction with the other forms of chart analysis described in Chapters 4 through 7. These angles— especially when a potential change in trend has been signaled—are useful in determining the slope of the incipient trend. The shallower the slope of the trend line, the less likely the new trend is to hold. The steeper the angle, the more likely it is to be the

FIGURE 10-2: Two-year daily chart of Intel (INTC)

beginning of a significant move. Gann's extensive views on trading and many of the topics discussed in the prior chapters are summarized in Gann's trading rules which are included in Chapter 11.

NOTES

1 Achelis, Steven B., *Technical Analysis From A to Z*, Irwin Professional Publishers, 1995, pg. 148.

2 Ibid., pg. 148

3 Ibid., pgs. 148-149

Gann's Twenty-Four "Never-Failing" Rules [1]

Gann always believed that in order to make a success at trading the markets, one must follow a series of well-defined rules, never once deviating from them regardless of circumstance. He provided 24 of his most reliable rules for the trader to follow in any market and in all circumstances. A list of his rules, along with the appropriate heading, follows.

1 Amount of capital to use. Divide your capital into 10 equal parts and never risk more than one-tenth of your capital on any one trade.

2 Use stop-loss orders. Always protect a trade when you make it with a stop-loss order 3 to 5 points away.

3 Never overtrade. This would be violating your capital rule.

4 Never let a profit run into a loss. After you once have a profit of 3 points or more, raise your stop-loss order so that you will have no loss of capital.

> Gann always believed that in order to make a success at trading the markets, one must follow a series of well-defined rules, never once deviating from them regardless of circumstance.

5 Do not buck the trend. Never buy or sell if you are not sure of the trend according to your charts.

6 When in doubt, get out, and don't get in when in doubt.

7 Trade only in active stocks. Keep out of slow, dead ones.

8 Equal distribution of risk. Trade in 4 or 5 stocks, if possible. Avoid tying up all your capital in any one stock.

9 Never limit your orders to fix a buying or selling price. Trade at the market.

10 Don't close your trades without a good reason. Follow up with a stop-loss order to protect your profits.

11 Accumulate a surplus. After you have made a series of successful trades, put some money into a surplus account to be used only in emergency or in times of panic.

12 Never buy just to get a dividend.

13 Never average a loss. This is one of the worst mistakes a trader can make.

14 Never get out of the market just because you have lost patience or get into the market because you are anxious from waiting.

15 Avoid taking small profits and big losses.

Of these 24 rules, Gann considered the rule concerning placing a stop-loss order the most important. Throughout his writings, he continually emphasized the importance of placing protective stops on all trades, reminding the reader that big losses are prevented this way and profits preserved.

16 Never cancel a stop-loss order after you have placed it at the time you make a trade.

17 Avoid getting in and out of the market too often.

18 Be just as willing to sell short as you are to buy. Let your object be to keep with the trend and make money.

19 Never buy just because the price of a stock is low or sell short just because the price is high.

20 Be careful about pyramiding at the wrong time. Wait until the stock is very active and has crossed resistance levels before buying more and until it has broken out of the zone of distribution before selling more.

21 Select the stocks with small volume of shares outstanding to pyramid on the buying side and the ones with the largest volume of stock outstanding to sell short.

22 Never hedge. If you are long of one stock and it starts to go down, do not sell another stock short to hedge it. Get out at the market; take your loss and wait for another opportunity.

23 Never change your position in the market without a good reason. When you make a trade, let it be for some good reasons or according to some definite plan; then do not get out without a definite indication of a change in trend.

24 Avoid increasing your trading after a long period of success or a period of profitable trades.

He also advised continually following up on a stop-loss order by adjusting it higher or lower, as the case may be, in order to further protect profits and guard against potential losses.

Of these 24 rules, Gann considered the rule concerning placing a stop-loss order the most important. Throughout his writings, he continually emphasized the importance of placing protective stops on all trades, reminding the reader that big losses are prevented this way and profits preserved. He often said that "failing to place a stop-loss order and overtrading have been the cause of over 90 percent of the failures in Wall Street." He also advised continually following up on a stop-loss order by adjusting it higher or lower, as the case may be, in order to further protect profits and guard against potential losses.

Along with the necessity of placing a stop-loss order, Gann also heavily emphasized the importance of not changing your mind when once you have committed to a trade. "Nine times out of ten," he wrote, "when once you place a stop-loss order, if you never cancel it, it will prove to be the best thing that ever happened, and the man who adheres to this rule will make a success."

Gann also urged his readers to heed nothing but the message of the market and to ignore what financial writers and advisors might be saying about the market. It is your trading decision based on your interpretation of the market that will make you money, not someone else's opinion, he said. "One of the main reasons why traders make losses is because they do not think for themselves and allow others to think for them and advise them, whose advice and judgment is no better than their own," he wrote.

On this same score he advised, "When you think the market is reaching bottom or top, you will find

Gann also heavily emphasized the importance of not changing your mind when once you have committed to a trade. "Nine times out of ten," he wrote, "when once you place a stop-loss order, if you never cancel it, it will prove to be the best thing that ever happened, and the man who adheres to this rule will make a success."

that seven times out of 10 you will be wrong. It is not what the market does today, nor what you think it is going to do, that is important; it is exactly what the indications are that it will do at a later date when you expect to make profits. Your object should be to keep right on the market. Go with the trend of the market. Study all the time to determine the correct trend. Do not think about profits. If you are right on the market, the profits will come. If you are wrong, then use the old reliable protector, the stop-loss order."

NOTES

1 Excerpted from *45 Years in Wall Street*, by W.D. Gann, Lambert Gann Publishing, Pomeroy, Washington, 1949, pg. 20.

CHAPTER 12

Conclusion

The trading methods and theories of W.D. Gann will forever change the way you view the stock and commodity markets. Whether you are a short-term "swing" trader or a long-pull investor, Gann's wisdom can profit all traders in any type of market environment.

One of the amazing things about Gann theory is that it can be as simple or as complex as the trader wishes it to be, depending on how deep one wishes to delve into Gann's writings. Gann left an impressive body of work behind, which ranges from the fairly simple and straight-forward (as revealed in his seminal work, *Truth of the Stock Tape*) to the arcane and highly complex (as revealed in his "Master" series of commodity timing courses). In writing this book, we have purposely overlooked such Gann techniques as his various squaring formulas, "master charts," interplanetary cycle analysis, etc. Instead, we have focused solely on the most basic and easy-to-understand aspects of his work and provided an introduction to Gann Angles. It is our opinion that this is where Gann's best contributions to understanding market behavior were made.

One of the amazing things about Gann theory is that it can be as simple or as complex as the trader wishes it to be, depending on how deep one wishes to delve into Gann's writings. In this book, we have focused solely on the most basic and easy-to-understand aspects of his work.

Probably the best information that can be gleaned from Gann's voluminous writings is found in his early work on using charts to identify areas of accumulation and distribution. Today this is known as "support and resistance" analysis, which all technical analysts now embrace. Gann's early work on this was as clear and lucid—not to mention as accurate—as any commentator you'll read on the subject. Best of all, Gann was able to confer his knowledge and techniques to students without the aid of trend lines and geometrical chart patterns; in fact, his earlier works have very few chart examples at all. So clear and straightforward was his teaching that he was able to confer his wisdom without the use of visual aids.

What market analysts both yesterday and today have always aimed to discover is the balance between supply and demand, i.e., whether the buyers (the "bulls") or the sellers (the "bears") are in control of a given market at a given time. This is what classical tape reading and technical analysis aim at discovering, but Gann's original method of arriving at this conclusion was so amazingly fresh and insightful that it remains unsurpassed for its accuracy and simplicity, even today. Gann, better than perhaps any other market writer, was and is the best teacher on how to read the tape.

This book should not be construed as summarizing the whole of Gann's teachings. For that, the reader must look elsewhere. Rather, this book should be read as an introduction to the many and varied forms of his technical analysis, but principally his

This book should by no means be construed as summarizing the whole of Gann's teachings. For that, the reader must look elsewhere. Rather, this book should be read as an introduction to the many and varied forms of his technical analysis, but principally his tape reading method.

tape-reading method. There are many fine works available today, which contain greater scope and depth on Gann's more refined forecasting techniques. Now that a foundation in Gann theory has been laid in this book, perhaps you, the reader, will want to further pursue these avenues.

If you come away with nothing else from reading this book, remember Gann's oft-repeated rule: "Always let the market (i.e., the chart or tape) guide your trading decisions." Never buck the trend; always go with it. Never trade without a stop-loss order. Never overtrade. Never commit more than one-tenth of your capital to any one trade. Follow these rules religiously and you will find success in the financial markets.

APPENDIX

Dictionary of Terms

accumulation

The first phase of a bull market. The period in which far-sighted investors begin to buy shares from discouraged or distressed sellers. Financial reports are usually at their worst and the public is completely disgusted with the stock market. Volume is only moderate but beginning to increase on the rallies.

accumulation/distribution

Momentum indicator that associates changes in price and volume. The indicator is based on the premise that the higher the volume that accompanies a price move, the more significant the price move.

advance/decline line

The advance/decline line is undoubtedly the most widely used measurement of market breadth. It is a cumulative total of the advancing/declining issues. When compared to the movement of the market index, the A/D line has proven to be an effective gauge of the stock market's strength. The A/D line has to confirm the market movements. The A/D line is calculated by subtracting the number of stocks which declined in price for the day from the number of stocks which advanced, and then adding this value to a cumulative total.

advisory services

Privately circulated publications which comment upon the future course of financial markets and for which a subscription is usually required. Evidence suggests that the advisory services, in aggregate, act in a manner completely opposite to that of the majority and therefore represent an indicator of a contrarian opinion. Advisory Sentiment Index = percentage of bullish market newsletter writers in relation to the total of all those expressing an opinion.

amplitude of cycle

Normally the amplitude of a cycle is a function of its duration; i.e., the longer the cycle, the bigger the swing.

arithmetic scale

All units of measure on an arithmetic scale are plotted using the same vertical distance, so that the difference in space between 2 and 4 is the same as that between 20 and 22. This scale is not particularly satisfactory for long-term price movements, since a rise from 2 to 4 represents a doubling of the price whereas a rise from 20 to 22 represents only a 10% increase.

bear market

Period in which there is essentially a long decline in prices, interrupted by important rallies, usually for a long time. Bear markets generally consist of three phases. The first phase is distribution, the second is panic and the third is akin to a washout. Those investors who have held on through the first two phases finally give up during the third phase and liquidate.

bear spreading

The short sale of a future or option of a nearby month and the purchase of a distant contract. (One notable exception to this principle in the traditional commodity markets is the precious metals group. Bull and bear markets in gold, silver and platinum are led by the distant months.)

bear trap
A signal which suggests that the rising trend of an index or stock has reversed, but which proves to be false.

bull market
A period in which prices are primarily rising, normally for an extended period. Usually, but not always, divisible into three phases. The first phase is accumulation. The second phase is one of a fairly steady advance with increasing volume. The third phase is marked by considerable activity as the public begins to recognize and attempt to profit from the rising market.

bull trap
A signal which suggests that the declining trend of an index or stock has reversed, but which proves to be false.

bull spreading
The purchase of a nearby futures/options contract and a short sale of a distant contract. In certain types of bull markets which are caused by a tightness in the supply/demand situation, the nearby contract months usually rise faster than the distant ones.

beta
Measurement of sensitivity to market movements. The trading cycle (four weeks) breaks down in two shorter alpha and beta cycles, with an average of two weeks each (Walt Bressert).

blow-offs
(Climatic top) A sharp advance accompanied by extraordinary volume; i.e., a much larger volume than the normal increase which

signals the final "blow-off" of the trend. This is followed either by a reversal (or at least a period of stagnation, formation or consolidation) or by a correction.

bond market sector

The bond market (i.e., the long end) has three main sectors, which are classified according to issuer.

- US government
- Tax-exempt issuers (i.e., state and local governments)
- Corporate issuers

breadth (market)

Breadth relates to the number of issues participating in a move. A rally is considered suspect if the number of advancing issues diminishes as the rally develops. Conversely, if a decline is associated with increasingly fewer falling stocks, it is considered to be a bullish sign.

breakaway gap

The hole or gap in the chart which is created when a stock or commodity breaks out of an area pattern (areas on the bar chart where no trading has taken place). This gap usually occurs at the completion of an important price pattern and usually signals the beginning of a significant market move. Breakaway gaps usually occur on heavy volume. More often than not, breakaway gaps are not filled.

breakout

When a stock or commodity exits an area pattern.

buying pressure

Buying or selling pressure is measured by volume indicators. It measures the strength of the buying or selling.

call options

Options which give the buyer the right to buy the underlying contract or stock, at a specific price, within a certain period, and which oblige the seller to sell the contract or stock for the premium received, before the expiration of the designated time period.

cash index

Index expressed in money. This is in contrast to futures prices.

channel lines

The channel line, or the return line as it is sometimes called, is a line parallel to the basic trend line. It is the line in a bull market which is drawn parallel to the basic uptrend line which connects the lows.

coils

Another word for a symmetrical triangle. A symmetrical triangle is composed of a series of two or more rallies and reactions in which each succeeding peak is lower than its predecessor, and the bottom of each succeeding reaction is higher than its predecessor.

commodity options

A commodity gives the holder the right, but not the obligation, to purchase (a call) or sell (a put) on an underlying futures contract at a specific price within a specific period of time.

composite market index

Composite average — A stock average comprised of the stocks which make up the Dow Jones Industrial Average (DJIA) and the Dow Jones Utility Average. Basically a market index composed of a selection of specific stocks.

confirmation

In a pattern, the confirmation is the point at which a stock or commodity exits an area pattern in the expected direction by an amount of price and volume sufficient to meet minimum pattern requirements for a bona fide breakout. This is also true for oscillators. To confirm a new high or a new low in a stock or commodity, an oscillator needs to reach a new high or low as well. Failure of the oscillator to confirm a new high or a new low is called divergence and would be considered an early indication of a potential reversal in direction.

congestion area

The sideways trading area from which area patterns evolve. Not all congestion periods produce a recognizable pattern however.

consolidation

Also called a continuation pattern, it is an area pattern which breaks out in the direction of the previous trend.

contrary opinion

A measure of sentiment is useful in assessing the majority view, from which a contrary opinion can be derived.

cycles

The prices of many commodities reflect seasonal cycles. Due to the agricultural nature of most commodities, these cycles are easily explained and understood. However, for securities, the cyclical nature is more difficult to explain. Human nature is probably responsible.

decennial pattern

A pattern first cited by Edgar Lawrence Smith. It is a ten-year pattern, or cycle of stock price movements, which has essentially repeated itself over a 58-year period. The decennial pattern can be of greater value if it is used to identify where the strong and weak points usually occur, and then to check whether other technical phenomena are consistent.

diffusion index

A diffusion index shows the percentage of indicators which are above their corresponding levels in a previous period. The indicators are the coincident economic indicators which tend to rise and fall coincidentally with the overall economy. These indicators thus provide a good approximation of the economy. For example: industrial production, consumer installment debt, the federal budget deficit and inflation.

discount rate

The discount rate is the rate at which banks can borrow directly from the Fed. The Fed can reduce bank reserves by raising the discount rate and expand reserves by lowering the discount rate. In practice, the discount rate has little actual influence on interest rates.

distribution

The first phase of a bear market. During this first phase far-sighted investors sense the fact that business earnings have reached an abnormal height and unload their holdings at an increasing pace.

divergence

Divergence refers to a situation in which different delivery months, related markets or technical indicators fail to confirm one another. Divergence is a valuable concept in market analysis and one of the best early warning signals for impending trend reversals.

diversification

Limiting risk exposure by spreading the investments over different markets or instruments. The more negative the correlation between the markets, the more diversified the risk.

dominant cycle

Dominant cycles continuously affect futures prices and can be clearly identified. These cycles are the only ones of real value for forecasting purposes. Most futures markets have at least five dominant cycles.

Long-term cycle ....two or more years in length
Seasonal cycle ....one year
Primary or intermediate cycle ....9 to 26 weeks
Trading cycle ....four weeks
Short-term cycle........................several hours to several days

Dow Theory

In 1897, Charles Dow developed two broad market averages. The industrial average included 12 blue-chip stocks and the rail average was comprised of 20 railroad enterprises. The Dow theory resulted from a series of articles published by Charles Dow in the Wall Street Journal between 1900 and 1902. The Dow theory is the forerunner to most principles of modern technical analysis.

Basic tenets of the Dow theory:
- the averages discount everything;
- the market has three trends: primary, secondary and minor
- major trends have three phases;
- the averages must confirm each other;
- volume must confirm the trend (volume must expand in the direction of the major trend);
- a trend is assumed to be in effect until it gives definite signals that it has reversed.

downtrend

The trend is simply the direction of the market. A downtrend is a trend which is marked by descending peaks and troughs; in other words, lower subsequent highs and lower lows. An uptrend would be defined as a series of successively higher peaks and troughs (higher highs and higher lows).

Elliott Wave

Theory of market behavior by R.N. Elliott.

Basic tenets of the Elliot Wave principle:
- pattern, ratio and time, in that order of importance;
- pattern refers to the wave patterns or formations that comprise one of the most important elements of the theory;
- ratio analysis is useful for determining retracement points and price objectives by measuring the relationship between the different waves;
- and time is used to confirm wave patterns and ratios.

Basic concepts of the Elliott Wave principle:
- action is followed by reaction;
- there are five waves in the direction of the main trend, followed by three corrective waves (5-3 move);
- a 5-3 move completes a cycle. The 5-3 move then becomes two subdivisions of the next higher 5-3 wave; and
- the underlying 5-3 pattern remains constant although the time span of each may vary.

envelopes

An envelope is comprised of two moving averages. One moving average is shifted upward and the second moving average is shifted downward. Envelopes define the upper and lower boundaries of a stock's normal trading range.

exhaustion gap

The gap that appears near the end of a market move. Towards the end of an uptrend, prices leap forward with a final gasp. However, this forward leap quickly loses ground, and prices decrease within a couple of days or a week. When prices close under this last gap, it is usually a clear indication that the exhaustion gap has made its appearance. This is a classic example of when the filling of a gap in an uptrend has very bearish implications.

exponential smoothing

The exponentially smoothed average assigns a greater weight to the more recent activity. It is, therefore, a weighted moving average. Mathematically, a single exponential smoothing is calculated as follows:

- $X = (C-Xp)K+Xp$
- X is exponential smoothing for the current period.
- C is closing price for the current period.
- Xp is exponential smoothing for the previous period.
- K is smoothing constant, equal to 2/n + 1 for Compu Trac and 2/n for Back Trac.
- n is total number of periods in a simple moving average, which is roughly approximated by X.

failures

Normally, a failure is when a completed pattern is not confirmed by the direction of the following move. The failure (in the Elliot Wave) shows a situation in which, in a bull market for example, wave 5 breaks down into the required five waves, but fails to exceed the top of wave 3.

fan lines

Fan lines are constructed as follows: Two extreme points are identified on the chart, usually an important top and bottom. A vertical line is then drawn from the second extreme to the beginning of the move. This vertical line is then divided by 38%, 50% and 62%, with lines drawn through each point from the beginning of the trend. These three lines should function as support and resistance points on subsequent reactions by measuring 38%, 50% and 62% Fibonacci retracements.

Fibonacci numbers

A number sequence rediscovered by Fibonacci. In Liber Abaci, the Fibonacci sequence is first presented as a solution to a mathematical problem involving the reproduction rate of rabbits. The number sequence presented is 1, 2, 3, 5, 8, 13, 21, 34, 55, 89, 114 and so on to infinity. In technical analysis, the Fibonacci numbers are used to predict or measure future moves in stocks or to predict retracement levels.

filter rules

The rule for confirming a breakthrough or a breakout. An example of a filter rule is the 3% penetration criterion. This price filter is used mainly for breaking off longer-term trend lines, but requires that the trend line be broken on a closing basis by at least 3%. The 3% rule does not apply to some financial futures, such as the interest rate markets. Another example is a time filter, such as the two-day rule.

flags (continuation pattern)

A flag looks like a flag on the chart. That is, it looks like a flag if it appears in an uptrend. The picture is naturally upside down in a downtrend. It might be described as a small, compact parallelogram of price fluctuations, or a tilted rectangle which slopes back moderately against the prevailing trend.

flow of funds

Flow of funds analysis refers to the cash position of the different groups, such as mutual funds or large institutional accounts. The thinking here is that the larger the cash position, the more funds which are available for stock purchases. While these forms of analysis are generally considered to be of secondary importance, it often seems that stock market technicians place more reliance on them than on traditional market analysis.

Gann Retracements

Gann divided price actions into eighths: 1/8, 2/8, . . . 8/8. He also divided price actions into thirds: 1/3 and 2/3:

1/8 = 12.5%
2/8 = 25.0%
1/3 = 33.0%
3/8 = 37.5%
4/8 = 50.0%
5/8 = 62.5%
2/3 = 67.0%
6/8 = 75.0%
7/8 = 87.5%
8/8 = 100.0%

The 50% retracement is the most important to Gann. Gann believed that the other percentages were also present in market action, but with diminishing importance.

gaps

Gaps are simply areas on the bar chart where no trading has taken place. In an uptrend, for example, prices open above the highest price of the previous day, leaving a gap or open space on a chart which is not filled during the day. In a downtrend, the day's highest price is below the previous day's low. Upside gaps are signs of market strength, while downside gaps are usually signs of weakness.

group rotation

The overall market consists of many stock groups which are a reflection of the companies making up the various segments of the economy. The economy, defined by an aggregate measure such as Gross National Product (GNP), is either rising or falling at any given time. However, there are very few periods in which all segments are advancing or declining simultaneously. This is because the economy is not one homogeneous unit. Group rotation is the rotation within the different groups of stocks depending on at which stage the economic cycle is at the moment.

hedging

To minimize risk and avoid speculation. Futures and options can be used for hedging.

high-low indicator

The new high-low cumulative indicator is a long-term market momentum indicator. It is a cumulative total of the difference between the number of stocks reaching a new 52-week high and the number of stocks reaching a new 52-week low. This indicator provides a confirmation of the current trend. Most of the time the indicator will move in the same direction as the major market indices. However, when the indicator and market move in opposite directions (divergence), the market is likely to reverse.

insiders

Any person who directly or indirectly owns more than 10% of any class of stock listed on a national exchange, or who is an officer or director of the company in question.

intermediate trend

An intermediate, or secondary, trend is the direction of the trend in a period from three weeks to as many months.

intra-day

A record of price data during the day, such as 15-minute bar charts. These intra-day charts are extremely important for the timing aspects of trading.

key reversal day

The term "key reversal day" is widely misunderstood. All one-day reversals are potential key reversal days, but only a few actually become key reversal days. Many of the one-day reversals represent nothing more than temporary pauses in the existing trend after which the trend resumes its course. The true key reversal day marks an important turning point, but it cannot be correctly identified as such until well after the fact; that is, not until after prices have moved significantly in the opposite direction from the prior trend.

Kondratieff cycle

The Kondratieff wave, a 54-year cycle, is named after a Russian economist. This is a long-term cycle identified in prices and economic activity. Since the cycle is extremely long term, it has repeated itself only three times in the stock market. The up-wave is characterized by rising prices, a growing economy and mildly bullish stock markets. The plateau is characterized by stable prices, peak economic capacity and strong bullish stock markets. The down-wave is characterized by falling prices, severe bear markets and often a major war.

limit move

A move limited by the uptick or downtick rule in commodity trading.

log scale

Prices plotted on ratio or log scales show equal distances for similar percentage moves. For example, a move from 10 to 20 (a 100% increase) would be the same distance on a log chart as a move from 20 to 40 or 40 to 80.

long-term cycle

A long-term cycle is basically two or more years in length.

major market trend

The major market trend is the primary direction of the market. The Dow theory classifies the major trend as being in effect for longer than a year. Futures traders would be inclined to shorten the major trend to anything longer than six months.

margin

This occurs when an investor pays part of the purchase price for a security and borrows the balance, usually from a broker; the margin is the difference between the market value of the stock and the loan which is made against it.

margin: commodities versus stocks

The most important difference between stocks and commodity futures is the lower margin requirements on stock futures. All futures are traded at a margin, which is usually less than 10% of the value of the contract. The result of these low margin requirements is tremendous leverage. Relatively small price moves in either direction tend to be magnified according to their impact on overall trading results.

margin debt

Debt caused by margin requirements.

market averages

In stock market analysis, the starting point of all market analysis is always the broad market averages, such as the Dow Jones Average or the Standard & Poor's 500 Index. A market average is usually an index of the most important stocks in the market or a broad market index that covers 98-99% of the market as a whole.

member short sale ratio

The member short sale ratio (MSR) is a market sentiment indicator which measures the short selling activity of the members of the New York Stock Exchange. "Members" trade on the floor of the exchange, either on their own behalf or for their clients. Knowing what the "smart money" is doing is often a good indication of the near-term market direction. The MSR is the inverse of the public short sale ratio.

minor market trend

The minor, or near-term, trend usually lasts less than three weeks and represents shorter-term fluctuations in the inter-mediate trend.

momentum indicator

The momentum indicator measures the amount a security's price has changed over a given time span. It displays the rate of change as a ratio.

most active stocks

The most active stocks are stocks which are traded the most over a certain period. Statistics on the most active stocks are published in the general press on both a daily and weekly basis. Usually the 20 most active stocks are recorded.

moving average

A moving average is the average of the closing prices of x periods added up and divided by x. The term "moving" is used because the calculation moves forward in time. Moving averages are used to help identify the different kinds of trends (short-term, intermediate medium, etc.).

A smoothing device with a time lag.

The moving average is one of the most versatile and widely used of all technical indicators. Because of the way it is constructed and the fact that it can be so easily quantified and tested, it is the basis for most mechanical trend-following systems in use today.

moving average crossovers

One method used by technicians in terms of moving averages. A buy signal is produced when the shorter average crosses above the longer-term moving average. Two popular combinations are the 5- and 20-day averages and the 10- and 40-day averages.

neckline

Support or resistance level in a Head & Shoulders pattern. The neckline connects the lows or highs of the "shoulders" depending on the situation (H & S bottom or top formation).

nominality

The principle of nominality is based on the premise that, despite the differences which exist in the various markets and allowing for some variation in implementing cyclical principles, there seems to be a set of harmonically related cycles which affect all markets. A nominal model of cycle lengths can be used as a starting point for any market.

odd-lot ratios

There are a few odd-lot ratios:
- Odd-lot balance index (OLBI)
- Odd-lot short ratio
- Odd-lot purchases/sales

The OLBI is a market sentiment indicator which shows the ratio of odd-lot sales to purchases (an "odd-lot" is a stock transaction of less than 100 shares). The assumption is that "odd-lotters," the market's smallest traders, do not know what they are doing. When the odd-lot balance index is high, odd-lotters are selling more than they are buying and are therefore bearish on the market. To trade contrarily to the odd-lotters, you should buy when they are selling.

on-balance volume

On-balance volume (OBV) is a momentum indicator which relates volume to price. The OBV is a running total of volume. It shows whether volume is flowing into or out of a security. When the security closes higher than the previous close, all of the day's volume is considered up-volume. When the security closes lower than the previous close, all of the day's volume is considered down-volume. The basic assumption in OBV analysis is that OBV changes precede price changes. The theory is that smart money can be seen as flowing into a security by a rising OBV. When the public then moves into a security, both the security and the OBV will surge ahead.

open interest

Open interest is the number of open contracts of a given futures or options contract. An open contract can be a long or short open contract which has not been exercised, or has been closed out or allowed to expire. Open interest is really more a data field than an indicator.

oscillators

Method of creating an indicator. The oscillator is extremely useful in non-trending markets where prices fluctuate in a horizontal price band, or trading range, creating a market situation in which most trend-following systems simply do not work that well. The three most important uses for the oscillator:

- The oscillator is most useful when its value reaches an extreme reading near the upper or lower end of its boundaries. The market is said to be overbought when it is near the upper extreme and oversold when it is near the lower extreme. This warns that the price trend is overextended and vulnerable;
- A divergence between the oscillator and the price action, when the oscillator is in an extreme position is usually an important warning signal; and
- Crossing the zero line can give important trading signals in the direction of the price trend.

overbought level

An opinion on the price level. It may refer to a specific indicator or to the market as a whole after a period of vigorous buying, after which it may be argued that prices are overextended for the time being and are in need of a period of downward or horizontal adjustment.

oversold level

An opinion on the price level. A price move that has overextended itself on the downside.

overowned stocks

A stock is overowned when fashion-conscious investors are all interested in buying a certain stock.

point & figure

Method of charting prices. A new plot on a P&F chart is made only when the price changes by a given amount. P&F charts are only concerned with measuring price. P&F charts are constructed using combinations of X's and 0's known as "boxes." The X shows that prices are moving up, the 0 that they are moving down. The size of the box and the amount of the reversal are important.

primary trend

This is the most important long-term trend. A primary trend usually consists of five intermediate trends. Three of the trends form part of the prevailing trend, while the remaining two run counter to that trend.

public/specialist short sale ratio

It measures the round-lot short selling by the public against the New York Stock Exchange specialists on the floor of the exchange. It pits the smart money against one of the least informed categories of market participants.

rally

A brisk rise following a decline or consolidation of the general price level of the market.

reaction

A temporary price weakness following an upswing.

relative strength (RS)

An RS line or index is calculated by dividing one price by another. Usually the divisor is a measure of "the market," such as the DJIA or the Commodity Research Bureau (CRB) Index. A rising line indicates that the index or stock is performing better than "the market" and vice versa. Trends in the RS can be monitored by moving average crossovers, trend line breaks, etc. in the same way as any other indicator.

resistance

Resistance is the opposite of support and represents a price level or area over the market where selling pressure overcomes buying pressure and a price advance is turned back. A resistance level is usually identified by a previous peak.

retracement

Retracements are basically countertrend moves. After a particular market move, prices retrace a portion of the previous trend before resuming the move in the original direction. These countertrend moves tend to fall into certain predictable percentage parameters. The best known application of this phenomenon is the 50% retracement. For example: a market is trending higher and travels from the 100 level to the 200 level. The subsequent reaction very often retraces about half of the prior move.

seasonal cycle

Seasonal cycles are cycles caused by the seasonal changes in the supply-demand relationship (caused by factors which occur at about the same time every year).

secondary trend

Secondary trends are corrections in the primary trend and usually consist of shorter waves that would be identified as near-term dips and rallies.

sentiment indicator

Indicators which measure the market sentiment, such as:

- Specialist Public Ratio
- Short Interest Ratio
- Insider Trading
- Advisory Services

short interest

The short interest is a figure published around the end of the month citing the number of shares that have been sold short on the NYSE.

speed resistance lines

Technique which combines the trend line with percentage retracements. The speed resistance lines measure the rate of a trend's ascent or descent (in other words, its speed).

stock index futures

Futures contract on indices.

support area

Support is a level or area on the chart under the market where buying interest is sufficiently strong to overcome selling pressure. As a result, a decline is halted and prices turn back up again. A support level is usually identified beforehand by a previous reaction low.

trend line

A trend line is a straight line drawn up to the right which connects important points in a chart. An up-trend line is a line which connects the successive reaction lows, a down-trend line connects the successive rally peaks.

upside/downside volume

Measurements of upside/downside volume try to separate the volume into advancing and declining stocks. By using this technique, it can be subtly determined whether accumulation or distribution is taking place.

volume

Volume represents the total amount of trading activity in that market or stock over a given period.

whipsaws

Misleading moves or breakouts.

Gann's Works

Truth of the Stock Tape

by W.D. Gann

Written by a legendary trader who is reputed to have made $50 million in the markets in his lifetime. This is one of Gann's most important works, written early in his career (1923). Gann covers many facets of trading in this book, such as preparation for trading, rules for successful trading and investing, tape reading, charts and their use, how to determine a change of trend, and many others. Students of his methods will learn much from this book.

$49.00   Item #T130x-11972   231 pages

Gann Master Course: Original Commodity Market Trading Course

by W.D. Gann

This is Mr. Gann's original Commodity Course! Others claim to sell "original" Gann courses, but beware of hype! Most of these people either sell courses that have been changed in some way, or sell separate pieces of the courses at a substantial profit to themselves. Our courses contain Mr. Gann's original materials in full, PLUS many other documents and materials we feel are important to the trader.

No other company can give you this amount of information for this value!

This is the same course Mr. Gann sold for $5,000 well over 50 years ago! It is a gold mine of information to understanding Mr. Gann's techniques. We are constantly researching the volumes of manuscripts and charts Mr. Gann left behind and have added several new things to the course in the last few years. However, we have not altered or changed any of the original text or materials!

$1295   Item #T130x-2520

Tunnel Thru the Air or Looking Back From 1940

by W.D. Gann

This is an interesting story entwining the stock and commodity markets with the nation's struggle leading to World War II. Gann wrote this book in 1927 yet he described the events leading up to, and during World War II, with uncanny parallels to the real thing. Many events, inventions, market panics and booms mentioned in this book actually came about in later years.

Mysterious as it is, the reader can still tell that is was written by W.D. Gann. Even with his imagination turned loose, his approach to the market is undeniable.

$49.00   Item #T130x-2508   418 pages   ISBN: 0939093057

Truth of the Stock Tape and Wall Street Stock Selector

by W.D. Gann

Truth of the Stock Tape: A Study of the Stock and Commodity Markets with Charts and Rules for Successful Trading and Investing

A practical book written by a successful Wall Street man who has proved his theory in actual trading. He writes from twenty years' experience and gives examples of his rules by the Case System.

This is the only book published covering the investment and speculative field of Cotton and Grain as well as Stocks. It is fully illustrated with 22 charts showing plainly the successful method of trading.

In four books under one cover:
- Book I   Preparation for Trading
- Book II   How to Trade
- Book III   How to Determine the Position of Stock
- Book IV   Commodities, including Cotton, Wheat and Corn

Wall Street Stock Selector

Brings *Truth of the Stock Tape* up to date — published in May 1930. It explains the 1929 bull market and the cause of the panic which followed and tells of the coming investors' panic. When you lose money trading in stocks, it is usually because you guess and gamble on hope, while the man who makes money has definite rules for trading. You need a Wall Street education and this book will give you more real market knowledge than you can obtain from any other source.

$49.00   Item #T130x-2503   436 pages   ISBN: 093909312X

45 Years in Wall Street

by W.D. Gann

Forty-five years of actual trading experience and market research by W.D. Gann have made this book possible. He writes from practical application and not theory.

You have the opportunity to draw on the experience of the man who wrote such widely read books as:

Truth of the Stock Tape (1932)
Wall Street Stock Selector (1930)
New Stock Trend Detector (1936)
How to Make Profits in Commodities (1941)

They have been acclaimed by readers throughout the United States and foreign countries as the best books ever written on the Stock and Commodity Markets.

In his latest book, *45 Years in Wall Street*, W.D. Gann gives new and up-to-date rules—never before published—which are practical and proven. This book gives you a real Stock Market education.

$49.00   Item #T130x-2504   148 pages

Trading Resource Guide
Tools for Success in Trading

Suggested Reading List

The Precision Profit Float Indicator
Powerful Techniques to Exploit Price and Volume
by Steve Woods

Discover a revolutionary new technical indicator that takes Gann analysis and applies it to today's trading markets. Outlined in easy-to-follow steps, with real-world examples, mastering the art of Float Analysis is a must for cutting-edge traders. Without the float, a price and volume chart is only two-thirds of the picture. See why guru Martin Pring calls it an "innovative indicator that all serious traders will want to familiarize themselves with to help determine the most effective buy and sell points for specific trades."

Lawrence McMillan says Steve Woods "has done a thorough job of investigating and describing this new area of technical analysis and I highly recommend adding it to your arsenal of trading indicators."

Other reviewers say *The Precision Profit Float Indicator* is . . .

"Taking the trading world by storm."

"A landmark concept."

". . . it pushes the boundaries of technical analysis one step further."

"It considers not only stock's price and volume, but factors in the number of shares being traded at any given time."

"A beautiful thing, and elegant concept."

$69.95   Item #T130x-11529   224 pages   ISBN: 188327284X

▲ ▲ ▲ ▲ ▲ ▲

These books along with hundreds of others are available at a discount from Traders' Library. To place an order or find out more,
Call 1-800-272-2855 *or visit our web site at*
www.traderslibrary.com

Pattern, Price & Time
Using Gann Theory in Trading Systems
by James A. Hyerczyk

'A thorough, comprehensive book, painstakingly researched, extensive in documentation, and meticulous in detail. A precise narrative of the trading strategies of an extraordinary forecaster of more than market movements.'

— Leslie Rosenthal, Managing Partner, Rosenthal Collins Group

In this authoritative text, expert technician James Hyerczyk presents a straightforward overview of Gann Theory, its basic principles, and its proper applications in creating profitable trading systems. Hyerczyk examines, in complete detail, such essentials as the Master chart, percentage retracements, minor trend indicators, swing chart and angles trading, and cycle dates. In addition, Hyerczyk includes clearly defined, practical guidelines for determining the best combinations of pattern, price, and time to initiate successful trades.

The only professional book to explain how to put Gann tools to practical use, *Pattern, Price & Time* explains how to incorporate these instruments into real-time trading systems for all the major markets, including commodities, financial futures, foreign currencies, and the S&P 500. It also outlines methods for integrating Gann Theory into modern computer charting techniques and systems using current software, such as TradeStation, SuperCharts, and Excel spreadsheets. *Pattern, Price & Time* offers a breakthrough look at Gann tools and their use in real-world trading systems, filling a longstanding void in Gann Theory literature. This is a must-read for anyone looking to thoroughly understand and successfully implement one of the most important and powerful forecasting methods in existence.

$59.95   Item #T130x-8438   320 pages   ISBN: 0471253332

Gann Made Easy

by William McLaren

This material is not so much a book, as a course, replete with charts and chart overlays. The first chapter in the course deals with the psychological disciplines needed for successful trading such as mastering Hope, Fear and Greed, and the discipline of placing a protective stop loss.

The next chapter, 'How Markets Move,' is a particularly important piece dealing with the different phases a market goes through, such as trend and counter-trend moves, tops and bottoms, as well as the sideways market.

Bill McLaren emphasizes, that it is vital to have these basic understandings of price movement which ". . . is the foundation of analysis and all else is built upon this knowledge."

The 'Squaring of Price and Time' is covered in depth by introducing the reader to the techniques used by Gann such as:

- Geometric charts
- Angles: 1x1, 2x1, 1x2, etc.
- Price Squares: The Square of 144; The Square of the Range; and more
- The Square of Nine, a spiral chart of nine that is "a valuable tool for trading and forecasting"
- Time cycles
- The Planets and Geometric Vibration

There are plenty of examples and charts to work with, as well as chart overlays like the Square of 90, the Square of 52 and also a copy of the 'Master Calculator' Square of 144 that Gann, himself, used.

$240.00   Item #T130x-2500   ISBN: 0961801808

▲ ▲ ▲ ▲ ▲ ▲

W.D. Gann Treasure Discovered
Simple Trading Plans for Stocks & Commodities

Author: Robert Krausz

A well-researched trading plan marks the difference between successful traders and the "wanna-be's." Here are trading plans that have been viable over the years. Covers entry/exit rules, risk management, profit objectives and new swing trading techniques.

Swing trading plans as they should be. Every entry and exit rule is clearly defined and fully back-tested. New concepts in money management, trailing stops and profit objectives are part of each plan.

Clear definitions are the essence of Krausz's approach to the markets. Every trade's result, and rule used, ties into the Daily Chart with a matching numbering system. You know when and why each trade occurred. The entire back-test is illustrated.

Thom Hartle, Editor of *Technical Analysis of STOCKS & COMMODITIES* magazine, comments: "If you've ever seen Robert Krausz speak, or ever read Jack Schwager's *New Market Wizards* or his articles from *STOCKS & COMMODITIES* magazine, you will know that Krausz had identified that the chief difference between the successful trader and the wanna-be is the lack of a thoroughly researched trading plan. But what exactly is a trading plan? Within these pages, you have the opportunity to learn and use a real trading plan — in fact, a plan that has shown remarkable viability over history. The plans offered within these pages cover all of the important conceptual issues of having defined entry and exit rules, risk management and profit objectives. In addition, Krausz introduces some new swing-trading techniques."

$161.80   Item #T130x-6640   390 pages

▲ ▲ ▲ ▲ ▲ ▲

Technician's Corner
Books by Martin Pring

How to Select Stocks
by Martin Pring

Learn the Top Down approach to find the best stocks by looking for the best sectors in the best groups — Even in a Bear Market

How to Select Stocks shows you that each bull and bear market experiences a complete rotation of individual industry groups. Knowing which groups are emerging as market leaders makes it easier to select promising stocks within these groups.

Pring explains the environment in which individual groups do well and how you can spot it. He also teaches you powerful technical concepts such as comparative relative strength. Using relative strength allows you to spot stocks that are likely to out-perform the market, optimizing the use of your valuable capital.

Also covered, is how divergences between the relative and absolute performance indicate, in advance, when a stock is likely to reverse trend. Identifying long-term reversals, using his KST indicator, helps put things into perspective so you can zero in on several short-term technical tools for more precise market timing.

$59.95   Item #T130x-12387

Martin Pring's Introduction to Technical Analysis
A CD-ROM Seminar & Workbook
by Martin Pring

The top expert gives you a one-on-one course in every aspect of technical analysis. This interactive guide explains how to evaluate trends, highs & lows, price/volume relationships, price pattern, moving averages, momentum indicators, and more. It's the user-friendly way to master technical analysis from an industry icon.

$49.95   Item #T130x-8521   304 pages   ISBN: 0070329338

Momentum Explained — Basic & Advanced

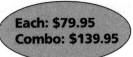

Each: $79.95
Combo: $139.95

*M*omentum Explained takes the foundation of *Martin Pring on Market Momentum* to create this 11-hour set of two tutorials on momentum and oscillator interpretation that goes beyond *Martin Pring on Market Momentum* as the "ultimate" momentum source, with 2 quizzes each.

Principles of Momentum Interpretation and Four Popular Indicators

Covers numerous techniques for interpreting momentum indicators, from overbought/oversold and divergences, to advance breakdowns and breakouts, extreme swings, mega overboughts and oversolds; how short-term momentum indicators can also be used to identify primary trend reversals, and why it is important, even for short-term traders, to know the direction of the main trend. Illustrated with marketplace examples using intraday, to long-term time frames, finer points of the RSI, Stochastic, MACD and Rate of Change indicators are discussed. For intermediate traders and above.

$79.00 Item #T130x-11933

Advanced Momentum Indicators

Explains the theory, methods of interpretation and strengths and weaknesses of a host of momentum indicators including the Directional Movement System, Parabolic, Commodity Selection Index, Chaikin Money Flow, Trix, Demand Index, Herrick Payoff, Volume Oscillator, Volume Rate of Change, Linear Regression, Indicator and Slope, Chaunde Momentum Oscillator (CMO), Dynamic Momentum Indicator, Relative Volatility Indicator, Relative Momentum Index, Klinger Oscillator, R-Squared Price Projection Bands and Oscillator, Inertia Forecast Oscillator, Qstick, Aroon. All in all, there are over 23 different indicators. For intermediate traders and above.

$79.00 Item #T130x-12388

Martin Pring's Introduction to Candlestick Charting

by Martin Pring

The integrity of the material is very sound and thoroughly researched—as we would expect from Martin Pring. At this price, the only question one must ask is why every trader's home hasn't got one yet. After all, even if you just want to gain an insight into the business of Japanese Candlestick Charting from an interested onlooker standpoint, you won't find a more accessible or better value means of gaining an in-depth tutorial on this fascinating oriental trading approach. Plaudits to Martin and Lisa Pring for producing such a sound piece of technical analytical tutorial.

Over 4 hours of multimedia, interactive instruction provides a solid grounding in this exciting field of technical analysis. All 10 chapters are complemented by colorful diagrams, animated theory reinforcements and real marketplace movies—so concepts are learned, applied and retained. An interactive quiz at the end of each chapter strengthens new skills and automatically keeps your current and two previous scores.

$69.95   Item #T130x-10251

Free 2-Week Trial Offer for U.S. Residents From Investor's Business Daily:

NVESTOR'S BUSINESS DAILY will provide you with the facts, figures, and objective news analysis you need to succeed.

Investor's Business Daily is formatted for a quick and concise read to help you make informed and profitable decisions.

To take advantage of this free 2-week trial offer, e-mail us at customerservice@traderslibrary.com or visit our web site at www.traderslibrary.com where you find other free offers as well.

Or call now:
1-800-272-2855 ext T130

Important Internet Sites

Traders' Library Bookstore . . . . **www.traderslibrary.com**
The #1 source for trading and investment books, videos and related products.

Active Trader . . . . **www.activetradermag.com**
Home page for Active Trader magazine, the only publication to focus exclusively on short-term trading

AIQ Systems . . . . **www.aiqsystems.com**
World leader in intelligent trading software

BigCharts.com . . . . **www.bigcharts.com**
A comprehensive and easy-to-use investment research web site providing access to research tools including interactive charts, quotes, industry analysis, market news and commentary. The site also features intuitive navigation and compelling graphics.

Bloomberg . . . . **www.bloomberg.com**
This major financial web site has it all—news, quotes, hot market information, lifestyle updates, investing tools, resources, and more. Turn to the industry leader for all your financial needs.

Bridge Financial . . . . **www.crbindex.com**
A comprehensive source of products and services for futures and options traders. This "onestop" site offers current quotes, online data, books, software products, news, and information from one of the world's leading financial information sources.

CandleCharts.com Inc. . . . . **www.candlecharts.com**
Leading candlesticks site from Steve Nison. Provides educational and advisory services combining candlesticks with western technical analysis.

Clif Droke. . . . . **www.tapetellsall.com**
This site contains a special section dedicated to forecasting markets using Elliott Wave Theory and also provides market commentary and forecasts based on principles from the author's books.

Dorsey Wright. . . . . **www.dorseywright.com**
The top source for information on Point & Figure analysis and comprehensive Point & Figure charts.

Equis. . . . . **www.equis.com**
Creators of MetaStock, the popular technical analysis software, this site offers a full range of powerful technical analysis tools for more profitable investing.

Equity Analytics. . . . . **www.eanalytics.com**
An excellent educational resource with extensive glossaries for technical analysis and many other topics.

Future Source. . . . . **www.futuresource.com**
A comprehensive source of information for futures and other traders providing futures quotes, settlement prices, charts, FWN news, chat rooms and other useful tools for traders of all levels.

Individual Investor. . . . . **www.individualinvestor.com**
News, quotes tools and columns plus articles from the Individual Investor magazine.

Martin Pring IIER. . . . . **www.pring.com**
This site is dedicated to teaching the art of technical analysis and charting.

Nirvana Systems. . . . . **www.omnitrader.com**
Creators of Omnitrader Software, the powerful trading software, this site provides a wide array of technical analysis and trading tools, including research and market updates, to help isolate the best trading opportunities.

Pristine.com. . . . . **www.pristine.com**
One of the world's largest and most sophisticated online educational services for active self-directed traders.

Track Data . . . . **www.tdc.com**
A supplier of electronically delivered financial data since 1981 with several services specifically designed to assist day traders. Timely market data, financial databases, historical information, data manipulation tools and analytical services are available.

About the Author

C LIF DROKE is a popular technical analyst, newsletter editor and author. He is the editor of *The Parabolic Report, Clif Droke's Internet Stock Outlook* and the *Gold Strategies Review*.

Gann Simplified is the fourth book he has authored in the Traders' Library Simplified Series. In the first book, *Technical Analysis Simplified,* Droke distills the essential elements of technical analysis into one powerful volume—covering all the basics: The Dow Theory, pattern recognition, volume, breadth, reliability of chart patterns, support and resistance, trend lines and channels, and one-day reversals. Martin Pring says *Technical Analysis Simplified* is "a great primer covering all the technical analysis basics every active investor needs to know."

In his second book, *Elliott Wave Simplified,* Droke takes the mystery out of using this effective technique—without being deluged with details. *Stocks & Commodities Magazine* says: "Hits the mark where most others on the subject fail . . . reveals a few new tricks even the advanced student will find useful." Included are the basics of technical analysis and R.N. Elliott's simple and proven theory, plus common pitfalls made when using Elliott Wave, as well as how the theory relates to trading volume, contrary opinion, channel analysis, the fan principle, filtered waves and more.

In the third book, *Moving Averages Simplified*, Droke's step-by-step approach takes you through every aspect of moving averages— from trading using single or double moving averages, to identifying price cycles and support and resistance levels. Ed Downs, founder of Nirvana Systems says, "I cannot recommend this book enough, and I give it four stars."

All four books are available at
www.traderslibrary.com

Notes:

Notes:

Notes:

Notes:

Notes:

Notes: